The Faithful Steward

31 DAYS OF PRAYER FOR THOSE WHO MANAGE THE RESOURCES OF OTHERS

CLAUDE BLANKENSHIP, CPA*

WITH PASTOR DAN SCOTT, DMIN

EDITED BY ELICIA HYDER

· INACTIVE-RETIRED

CPA
PRAYER
ALLIANCE

Contents

Dedication

In honor and memory of my mother, Allie Baker Blankenship; and A.S. and Mildred Bailey, who were surrogate parents to me.

SPECIAL THANKS

I also want to thank Pastor Dan Scott, publishing consultant Elicia Hyder, and CJ and Amanda Blankenship for bringing this book to life.

Foreword

BY CJ BLANKENSHIP

Over the course of our lives, there are precious few people we come to know in fine detail, or in ultra-high 8K definition as we might say in our current digital age. Claude Blankenship is one of those limited individuals in my life.

This intimate knowledge is not just derived from his role as my father. It developed over decades of daily mentorship in the CPA profession and throughout our business partnership at the public accounting firm and in related ventures.

When we watch an old classic movie that has not been remastered, it doesn't seem to quite add up to our recollection. Pictures that were clear in our minds and sounds that were crisp are muted and muffled. Their reproduction doesn't match our memory. We are not able to see the real thing. It is not that they have lost their luster over time; it is that our ability to capture what was there and reproduce it has improved or, in the case of remastering, has evolved. We are able to feel closer to the clarity of real life.

We can see things as though we are there in the room, as though we are there in person. It is not a flawed reproduction or a faulty recollection. It is crisp and clear.

I have been there with my father. I have seen the real picture and heard the true audio. My recollection isn't a reproduction that has been shared with me or remastered by others. I know Claude Blankenship, in the finest detail. Good and bad!

It would be impossible to reproduce all the stories of the lives Dad has touched, the businesses he has helped, the families that have been transformed over a sixty-year career in accounting and business. Dad has been retired for years, and still hardly a week passes where I don't cross paths with a businessperson who has a story about my father.

These stories usually begin with a difficult moment in their lives that somehow led to an interaction with Claude. They then conclude with an emotional recounting of the spiritual or personal insights that he shared with them, and the beneficial, life-changing impact that pivotal meeting had on the trajectory of their life.

This has often transpired in the hardest of personal seasons. And while many of these stories have an economic vein, a disproportionately high number have less to do with money and more to do with the heart and the struggles of living in a fallen world with fellow fallen people who have yet to be restored—or remastered, if you will.

I know what this looks like, personally, because I have experienced it as well. In my youth, I walked away from the faith and nearly everything else in my life. I ultimately fell into a deep depression of drug and alcohol addiction. Through those hard years, I recall hearing about Dad meeting with a fellow believer every Wednesday night. Together, they prayed that I would not only find sobriety, but that I would come back to the faith.

Dad knew that his call to steward me as his child was rooted in realizing that he couldn't change me as much as he longed to see me changed. I was not his to change. I was his to steward. He knew that the power of prayer and the faithfulness of love would be the only things that could bring about transformation.

And they did.

Not only have I been sober for nearly 25 years, but for most of them, Dad and I have worked together every day. He has been teaching me to faithfully steward our clients, our people, our business, and God's resources each step along the way.

This is what being a faithful steward is all about.

We survey the landscape of the people, the places, and the precious and fleeting moments of our lives. After close observation, we are called to wholeheartedly embrace those moments, engage with the requisite people, and channel the professional and spiritual wisdom that comes from the true Counselor.

Wisdom and insight dwell within us through the presence of the Holy Spirit, and we become more in tune to this divine direction through prayer. When Dad and I have faced hardship, challenge, and opportunity, we have been intentional about stopping to pray.

At a Christ-based recovery non-profit, where my father and I have served together for almost two decades, we teach men and women that early in every day—and early in every situation we encounter—to seek the Lord through Bible study, prayer, and worship.

It changes everything when we approach God first and work to understand His plan. Or, more appropriately, invite Him to show us His will, or impact the situation at hand.

These prayers for faithful stewards help financial professionals gain an understanding of God's perspectives that He has shared with us on so many topics. But they are not just for spiritual financial professionals who are stewarding their client's assets, they pertain to all of us.

Everything we have is ours only for a season. Just as we are here today and gone tomorrow, the assets we steward are only temporarily in our hands. They ultimately belong to someone else. And as such, we will give a final accounting of how we handled that which we were entrusted with. This is not an annual review for your job, or a seasonal review for a promotion. This will be an eternal review of how we handled our entire lives, including not just our work but also our families, our faith, our time, God's money, and the pivotal moments of decision and potential impact that we come across nearly every day. In both the big moments and the small ones, we are called to faithfully steward all we have been blessed to encounter.

Whether you are managing other people's wealth at a financial firm, or answering the phone of a home-repair company, or pouring coffee at the local bistro to feed the caffeine dependent engine of businesses (our firm wouldn't survive without coffee service!), or whether you are a CPA helping business owners with accounting and sound decision-making—in all our jobs, we are called to carefully care for these assets. Time, perhaps being the most precious.

Claude has consistently done this well. And he has taught others to do the same, including me.

When you interact with my father, you feel his genuine love and care for you, as though you are the most important thing in the world to him in that moment. Because you are. All we have in this world is the moment and what it holds, and my father has taught me to steward that well by his example.

I would be remiss not to share one closing thought about Claude Blankenship.

My father began his journey in abject poverty as one of 12 children in the *hollers* of West Virginia. He had basically never left the county. He had no indoor plumbing until adulthood. What followed were the days of "wine and roses" and great worldly success. Then he lost it all through no direct fault of his own. Through everything, Dad has modeled one characteristic that moves my heart and soul above all others: Claude Blankenship has an almost infinite capacity for hope.

When his financial world was falling apart around him, his family was broken, and he didn't know if God would provide for his next meal—let alone the next mortgage payment—Claude Blankenship never gave up hope.

Perhaps, this is the thing he has faithfully stewarded the best in his life. He has fervently held onto, and taught me, to never give up hope. And he has taught countless others to do the same.

His beautiful capacity for hope is rooted in his prayer life. Hope and prayer go hand in hand. Prayer renews our hope while the world works to erode it.

You see, the person who fails to hold on to hope, is hopeless. And when one becomes hopeless, their effectiveness, their energy, and the results of their lives are rendered nearly useless.

One can't help but attribute a meaningful percentage of our society's current pandemic of depression to a lack of hope or loss thereof. The truth is that many of us have lost our Source of hope.

If only I could be as full of hope as my dad. Hope is infectious. And hope sustains. We all should strive to be harbingers of hope.

I will close with this quote from F. Scott Fitzgerald in *The Great Gatsby*. This classic examination of misgivings and character, attempts to describe what happened in the tragedy that unfolded. More specifically, why Gatsby was so infectious. Why people loved him. What led to his success.

My dad is loved by so many and has experienced what some might call worldly success. What I care about is his spiritual success. Over the years, I have thought of this quote when thinking about his personality and the natural gifts God gave him:

> *"If personality is an unbroken series of successful gestures, then there was something gorgeous about him, some heightened sensitivity to the promises of life, as if he were related to one of those intricate machines that register earthquakes ten thousand miles away . . . it was an extraordinary gift for hope, a romantic readiness such as I have never found in any other person and which it is not likely I shall ever find again."[1]*

F. Scott Fitzgerald, *The Great Gatsby*

As you interact with the true Source of our collective hope, and you steward the resources that you have been entrusted with daily (regardless of what they may be), it is my hope that these lessons and prayers help you experience the counsel of Christ as Paul revealed to us in Romans.

All this earth and everything in it is the Lord's. He specifically designed, created, and placed us here to enjoy it, steward it, and realize that it is not ours but His, and for His glory!

Steward well.

> *Oh, the depth of the riches and wisdom and knowledge of God! How unsearchable are his judgments and how inscrutable his ways!*
> *"For who has known the mind of the Lord,*
> *or who has been his counselor?"*
> *"Or who has given a gift to him*
> *that he might be repaid?"*
> *For from him and through him and to him are all things. To him be glory forever. Amen.*

Rom. 11:33–36, ESV

Introduction

BY CLAUDE BLANKENSHIP, CPA*

I began thinking about how to minister to certified public accountants on a Thursday, in May 2015. One of my clients had been killed in a car wreck. He was seventy-five.

The news was sobering. A couple of weeks before, I had turned seventy-five.

I was already aware that I had entered a new season of life. So, the death of that client was like an underlined sentence in a book: <u>Pay attention.</u>

My wife, Candace, had recently said that since I was still

attending all the conventions and chapter meetings of our CPA society, I should find something "older men can do."

I had laughed and asked her (and myself), "Well, what *do* old men do?"

The answer came during the annual convention of Tennessee Certified Public Accountants in June of that same year. I had driven to Knoxville thinking about how to fit in.

At the opening dinner, a man was saying the blessing. He added a petition for divine comfort for the family of a man who had died a few days before—someone who had planned to be at that very convention.

When the prayer concluded, I turned to a neighbor and asked, "How did that man die?"

Another car wreck.

Life is uncertain, I thought. *I must make it count.*

After the convention, my thoughts about cultivating the spiritual lives of accountants began taking shape. So did the answer to my wife's remark about doing what "older men can do."

Older people could pray.

I decided to ask CPAs sixty-five and older to meet once a month to pray for our profession, its members, and their families. We would pray for our country, state, and counties. We would pray for the nation's president, congresspersons, senators, and judges.

I would also ask the Chapter President of the state of Tennessee to find volunteers to pray for thirty minutes before the beginning of each of our meetings.

My thoughts were getting clearer about what to do. God had been preparing me to do this work for a long time.

Years before, I had served on the Board of Directors for the American Institute of Certified Public Accountants. After speaking at one of its conventions, a CPA from Colorado suggested I start an Association of Christian Accountants in my state.

Now, after the death of that client and the conference in Knoxville, I knew it was time.

I obtained a Tennessee charter for The Certified Public Accountants Prayer Alliance, and at the time of this writing, I am seeking approval from the Internal Revenue Service and the state of Tennessee for not-for-profit status.

I have done these things because I believe that CPAs who seek the Lord will make a difference: in their personal lives, in our profession, and in the lives of all those they serve.

Second Chronicles 7 says that when people turn from their wicked ways and repent of their sins, the Lord forgives them and heals their nation. Responding to the challenges of our times requires discernment, wisdom, and courage. These are spiritual qualities that come from outside us—from the One who made us.

In other words, there is no better time to start a ministry for financial workers.

The prophet Micah (7:7) says that always God hears our prayers and answers them according to his perfect will. That implies that God will undergird the work we are *called* to do, if we but ask.

For many of us, managing the material resources of others is not merely an occupation. It is a *vocation*. The word is derived from the Latin *vocare*, meaning "to call." A vocation, like an occupation, is often the source of our income.

However, experiencing accounting as a vocation means that we experience this work as a responsibility not only to our clients or the law, but to the Lord. That transforms accounting into something much more than merely a practical way to make a living. It becomes the context in which (and through which) we develop our spiritual lives.

The Biblical term for this view of our work is *stewardship*. A steward is a man or woman called to manage the resources of another person.

Naturally, if "the earth is the Lord's and all it contains," then in a sense, all of us are stewards. In the opening words of Genesis, we learn that all human beings are responsible for how they manage the earth and its resources. Faithful stewardship of the material world results in various levels of financial flourishing, which leads to an accumulation of goods and to personal influence within the social world.

The Bible teaches that God cares about how we manage these things on behalf of ourselves and others. Therefore, it's important that as we grow financial capacity, we also develop the ethics, morals, and legal knowledge required for managing it well.

This is where accountants and other kinds of financial workers fit into the work of stewardship. They focus on the material flourishing of others within legal, ethical, and moral parameters. For biblically centered people, this kind of stewardship requires spiritual development as well as legal and financial knowledge.

That is why financial work is more than a means of making a living. It is a spiritual practice, an important means through which God forms our hearts. The apostle Paul said that the central characteristic of a godly steward is faithfulness. As we become trustworthy advisors to our clients, helping them manage and develop their resources legally, morally, and ethically, we glorify God.

We also develop our own character.

Few of us keep these things in mind in the day-to-day. We are easily sidetracked. We are often focused on ourselves. Even if we care deeply about being godly stewards, we rarely remain focused on that lofty ideal—especially during tax season!

That is why I wrote this book.

It is a collection of prayers and meditations gleaned from my career as an accountant. Like you, dear reader, I have had to fight to remain focused on the spiritual nature of our work. However, during challenging times, I cried out to the Lord.

You can learn to do that for yourself.

I encourage you to begin your morning or end the day with one of the short prayers and reflections in this book. You can add your requests for guidance and provision.

These brief times of reflection, I believe, will become indispensable for starting or ending your day.

I have tried to make these reflections relevant to younger people. However, these meditations have emerged from my life, and an important component is my age. The hymns I learned as a child, the books I have read, and even the translation of the Bible I have used, belong to another era. I decided to include those dated aspects of my journey, not because they are superior in any way to contemporary songs and books, but because they have been the influences that molded me.

Hopefully, you will experience these old references as something like the snapshots in your grandparents' photo albums. Like the uncles, aunts, cousins, and neighbors that once populated your grandparents' world, the hymns and references of my earlier years will perhaps feel endearing and instructive for how your own life can unfold.

Most of all, I pray that my reflections will encourage you to think about the spiritual legacy you are building, and which one day you will offer to others.

Claude Blankenship
Brentwood, Tennessee
June 1, 2024

*Inactive-Retired

Prayer

1

Our Father which art in heaven, hallowed be thy name, thy kingdom come, thy will be done in earth as it is in heaven, give us this day, our daily bread...

Matthew 6: 9–11, KJV

Prayer is the heart of spiritual life.

You know that already.

Likely, you assume that you don't pray very much or very well.

Please don't let this intimidate you.

Rabbi Abraham Joshua Heschel once said that we all pray more than we think. Every attempt to talk to God, he said, however feeble—whether our words are formal or informal, whether we are silently respectful or spouting words that make little rational sense, or whether we are simply expressing a spiritual awareness through a physical gesture—is prayer (Heschel, *Man's Quest for God*)[1].

"God," said William Cowper, "is his own interpreter" (Cowper, *God Moves in a Mysterious Way*)[2].

That said, most of us look for a kind of "spiritual home

plate," a place from which to begin our prayer. We want an anchor to which we can attach our spiritual experience.

That is why we begin this book with the *Lord's Prayer*, or, as some believers call it, the *Our Father*.

Whatever we call it, it is the model prayer for Christians. Interestingly though, if you are not a Christian, you will not likely find any part of this prayer offensive. Jews and Muslims, for example, can pray this prayer without any sense of compromise to their own beliefs about God.

You don't have to be a Christian to learn and use this prayer. It is for everyone.

Even if we're uncertain about our religious path but have a vague desire for some sort of spiritual life, the Lord's Prayer is a wonderful place to begin.

That is why Jesus gave it to us.

Most people reading this book can probably recite the Lord's Prayer. It is, after all, the most familiar set of words in Western literature. That is all the more reason we should reflect on what its words mean.

Familiarity sometimes diminishes the meaning of well-known words. Reflection can make them new again.

Jesus taught us to recite this prayer because his disciples asked him to teach them how to pray. It is, therefore, a kind of outline of all of Christ's teachings about spiritual life.

The first word in this prayer is "Our."

Notice that the word is *not* "My."

Jesus wants us to begin our spiritual life aware that God is "*Our*" Father. Prayer connects us with everyone else who prays. Even if we are alone or in private, prayer begins with the awareness of a vast multitude of spiritual siblings, scattered throughout all times and space, seeking to know the same Creator.

Although the spiritual path is personal, it is not solitary. As the famous hymn says, *"Brothers, we are treading where the saints have trod"* (*Brethren, We Have Met to Worship,* Askins)[3].

Calling God "Father," acknowledges Him as the source of all things, visible and invisible. It reminds us that before He created the universe, God had each of us in mind. He cares about how we each fit into creation and into the community of everyone who acknowledges Him.

The word *hallowed* is older than the English language. The only related word that has endured in contemporary English is Halloween! The connection between these two words is the sense of awe, otherness, and godly fear.

Reverence, awe, and wonder are the markers of intentional, focused prayer. Although the One whom we hallow—or treat as holy—is a loving Father, awareness of God's mysterious and unimaginable glory arouses our hearts in ways nothing else does. That is why prayer begins by deliberately stepping into wonder, by *hallowing* the name of God.

In that attitude of awe and reverence, we pray that God's purpose prevails not only in the mysterious realms beyond us, but in the everyday world around us. We ask, in other words, that our everyday lives and work will reflect submission to God and to the ways of God.

Jesus tells us to express our confidence that the almighty God, the heavenly Father, will provide everything we need. Although our most important need is the healing of our soul, it is difficult to focus on our soul when we are hungry or lack shelter. So, we pray for "bread," the symbol of material sustenance of all kinds.

Having sufficient food and shelter, we can attend to our soul.

The Scriptures tell us that if we believe in our hearts and confess with our tongues that Jesus is the Son of God, we will have eternal life. That doesn't mean merely living forever. It means living differently.

Eternal life is an entirely different kind of living. Jesus called it *abundant* life.

This abundant life gradually shapes our personality and character. As we lean into it, it forms us into the persons God intended us to be.

PRAYER:

Lord,

Like your first disciples, I want to know how to pray. Like the apostle Paul, I confess that I do not know how to pray as I should.

Help me pray this model prayer you gave to us. Help me pray it in those times when I can have nothing else to say. Help me pray it when my words seem inadequate.

As I pray it, may it colonize my soul, teaching me to focus on what concerns you and to turn from those things that do not, so that by internalizing these holy words, I may learn to glorify you in this life as I prepare for the life to come.

Amen

REFLECTION:

_____

_____

_____

_____

_____

_____

_____

_____

_____

Practice

2

Forgive us our debts, as we forgive our debtors. Lead us not into temptation but deliver us from evil; for thine is the kingdom and the power, and the glory, for ever. Amen.

Matthew 6:12–13, KJV

There are thousands of books on the *Lord's Prayer*. Many of them are thick and dense, filled with footnotes and references. These can help us think through the theological implications of this prayer.

The goal is to develop a habit of prayer. We want to learn to pray often and from our hearts. That is why Jesus gave us these words to pray. When we recite them with intention and reverence, they can open our souls to God's presence, guidance, and provision. They thrust us into a journey with God and toward God.

Unfortunately, our journey will face resistance.

The Lord's Prayer warns us that sin and evil oppose our spiritual lives. That is why we ask for forgiveness for our sins and deliverance from evil.

We think and do wrong things.

We fail to do things that we should.

We also suffer from false guilt, when we feel responsible for things beyond our control.

The guilt and shame caused by real and imagined wrong-doing are heavy burdens. They restrict our joy. They diminish our fruitfulness in the world.

We need a way to unburden ourselves of all this shame and guilt. That is why the apostles talked about the "gift of repentance."

Knowing we have been forgiven, we can experience God's presence as the source of life and joy. We become life-giving to others.

We flourish.

The Lord's Prayer not only teaches us to ask forgiveness for ourselves. It tells us to forgive those who have harmed us. Forgiving others removes a great hindrance to our spiritual lives. As we forgive others, we grow more certain of God's forgiveness toward us.

If we do not forgive others, Jesus said, God will not forgive us.

That is a serious warning.

Of course, it's sometimes difficult to forgive others. Sometimes, the hurt others have caused us is intense. We can't rise above it without help. However, God's mercy triumphs over justice, which gives us hope for ourselves. Asking God to help us forgive others is a way to participate in God's nature. A sincere desire to forgive becomes an authentic part of our character.

Most of the time, our difficulty forgiving others is because we have a bruised ego. We are wounded because we believe we have lost face or have been disrespected. The Bible teaches us to deal with this sense of loss by "considering others as more important than ourselves."

This is not because God wants us to belittle ourselves, but because God wants to heal us from these heavy burdens. When we accept God's forgiveness and then forgive others, we experience what the Scripture means when it says, "The one whom the Son has set free, is free indeed." (John 8:36)

The Bible says that we are infected with a deadly spiritual disease called sin. This illness distorts our desires, provoking us to hunger for things that do us harm. When we desire to do good, sin hinders us from doing it. If we intend to live a spiritual life, then we must find healing for our souls. According to the New Testament, this healing begins with repentance and trust in God's forgiveness.

Spiritual life is the process through which this healing continues throughout this life and into the life to come.

Another spiritual force that hinders our journey toward God is called evil. Unlike sin, which comes from within us, evil comes from outside us. Moreover, it is not merely a force, but a personality. Most scholars believe that is what Jesus had in mind because in many of the most ancient texts, the prayer asks for deliverance from the *Evil One*.

Evil takes advantage of our weaknesses, the "sins that so often beset us," as the Epistle to the Hebrews puts it. In other words, evil exploits our brokenness. That's what we mean by temptation. The reason we're not always strong enough to resist temptation is because they come in a form tailor-made for us.

Temptation is not a sin, though. We should never despair simply because we struggle with temptation. The struggle is, in fact, evidence that God is working in us. Otherwise, we would not resist temptation. We wouldn't fret because we find it attractive. We would simply give into it without any fuss.

We need wisdom to recognize temptation for what it is—an attempt by evil to undermine our spiritual life.

We also need the power to escape it, which comes from the

power of the Holy Spirit. The forces of evil are craftier and stronger than us. However, as the old Gospel song says, "I am weak but thou art strong." [1]

We usually end the Lord's prayer with the traditional phrase: "For Thine is the kingdom, and the power, and the glory forever." That was not originally part of the prayer as Jesus taught it. It has become so familiar over the centuries though that it seems strange to omit it. Besides, the little doxology reminds us that cultivating spiritual life is rooted in our reliance on the Lord.

We have no kingdom, power, or glory. We are at best, stewards of what has been given us to manage. That includes our spiritual resources.

For years, I have said the Lord's Prayer every night before I go to bed. I recite it again as I arise each morning.

This habit of praying the Lord's Prayer has led to spontaneous prayers erupting from inside my soul throughout the day. Slowly, this prayer has enabled me to keep turning toward the Holy Spirit, the Lord, the Giver of Life.

I encourage you to consider adopting this spiritual practice.

PRAYER:

Lord,

Almighty God, help me to persistently pray the words our Lord Jesus Christ taught us. And as I lift them before You, let their meaning take root in my heart, shaping my desires until my whole life is conformed to Your ways.

Teach me to seek that which is pleasing in Your sight and to pray aright, that I may ever grow into the likeness of Him who has redeemed me, through Jesus Christ our Lord.

Amen

REFLECTION:

_____
_____
_____
_____
_____
_____
_____
_____
_____
_____
_____
_____
_____
_____
_____
_____
_____
_____
_____
_____
_____
_____
_____
_____
_____
_____
_____
_____
_____
_____

Consistency

3

The prayer of a righteous man availeth much.

James 5:16, KJV

My spiritual life first developed around the King James Version of the Bible. However, many of my readers may be unfamiliar with its old words and phrases.

The word *avails* may be one of those. It means advantageous or effective.

The apostle James adds that our prayer should be fervent, intense, and persistent.

For James, prayer is not merely a pious exercise unrelated to everyday life. It is an expression of spiritual intimacy, an ongoing connection between our souls and our God. Sincere and heartfelt prayer is a means through which God enables profound change, both in the one who prays and the part of the world that a praying person influences.

Later, we will see how important this is for those who work with financial resources. Money has great power, both to bless and destroy. That is why stewards often gain considerable influence in the lives of others. If that influence is to be wholesome and life-giving, the steward must continually turn to God.

James seems to see prayer not only as a personal connection between an individual and God but also as a bond that connects all those who pray to one another. He views this bond as a means of healing, which is why he urges us to confess our faults *to* one another and to pray *for* one another. He insists that this intercessory prayer causes positive change to occur in the world.

As people who advise clients, whether as certified public accountants, working as chief financial officers, mortgage lenders, or in any of the other ways we care for the finances of others, we become responsible for making difficult decisions. Coworkers and employees, along with our clients, may seek our advice. How (and why) we approach such situations is often as important as any advice we offer. Prayer not only opens our minds to divine guidance in these occasions, it softens our attitudes toward those we serve.

Gradually, prayer can become a natural rhythm of who we are, like breathing. That is what the apostle Paul had in mind when he said that we should pray without ceasing (1 Thessalonians 5:17.) He was implying that prayer should permeate every part in our life, whether personal or professional.

In some situations, this habitual prayer becomes fervent and insistent.

Jesus talks about that in a story about a woman and an unjust judge.

The woman kept followed the crooked judge around, promising to give him no peace until he made a righteous judgment. Jesus said we should pray like that woman, intently seeking and petitioning God to answer our prayer.

Intense prayer is not about getting God's attention, of course. If God notices a sparrow falling from the sky, we already have God's attention. No, intense prayer can create a shift in the deepest parts of our soul, preparing us to receive God's answer and to participate in whatever way God indicates.

Hearing stories about how prayer has worked in the lives of others helps us cultivate lives of prayer. They remind us that prayer changes things. They encourage us to believe that our prayer may be the means God uses to change us, and then, through us, change the situations we face.

When the founding leaders of the United States were drafting the Declaration of Independence, they couldn't agree on how to conclude it. Legend has it that Benjamin Franklin asked the delegates to pause their deliberations and seek the Lord for wisdom and guidance.

After praying, the delegates quickly finished the document.

Here is another story from the Bible.

> In those days Hezekiah was sick and near death. And Isaiah, the prophet, son of Amos, went to him, and said to him, thus says the Lord: "Set your house in order, for you will die, and not live."
>
> Then he turned his face toward the wall and prayed to the Lord, saying "Remember now, O Lord, how I have walked before you, in truth, and with the loyal heart, and have done what was good in your sight." And Hezekiah wept bitterly.
>
> Before Isaiah had gone out into the middle court, the word of the Lord came to him, saying, "Return and tell Hezekiah, the leader of My people, "Thus says the Lord, the God of David, your father: "I have heard your prayer, I have seen your tears; surely, I will heal you. On the third day you are go up to the house of the Lord and I will add to your days fifteen years.
>
> I will deliver you and this city from the hand

of the king of Assyria, and I will defend this city for My own sake and for the sake of my servant David."

2 Kings 20: 1-6, ESV

As our spiritual journey continues, we learn to pray about everything. We can begin our day breathing a prayer for our families, our churches, our workplace, our government—for whatever the Holy Spirit brings to our attention. Then, as the day continues, short prayers continue to express our concerns to God.

Slowly, we learn how to listen for God's guidance and to expect God's provision.

PRAYER:

Heavenly Father,

Grant me a heart to keep praying when the answer seems distant and unlikely. Guide me to amend my prayer, that it may come to reflect your will. Engage my heart, lest my prayer become empty clichés and cold declarations.

Help me to persist in prayer in everything that pleases you, that I not lose heart and fail to participate in the work you have assigned me. For the sake of Christ who saved me and the Holy Spirit who empowers me, I ask these things.

Amen.

REFLECTION:

_____

_____

_____

_____

Gratitude

4

"Blessed are You, Lord our God, King of the universe, who brings forth bread from the earth."

Baruch Ata

The traditional Jewish blessing over food is called the *Baruch Ata*, after its first two words in Hebrew. It acknowledges God as the source of all material provision and sustenance. It has been so commonly used in Jewish life that early Christians adapted it for consecrating bread and wine for the Communion service.

It's interesting that in this prayer we bless the Lord rather than the food. That implies that our material resources emerge from an immaterial source. It is neither our gold nor good ideas that create capital, but God working through the world—and through us.

We sometimes become anxious about our resources. When the stock market is down, jobs are scarce, interest rates are high, or we face any one of the many economic factors that cause us concern, blessing the Lord, the King of the universe, reminds us that the Creator notices even a sparrow that falls from the sky.

He knows what is going on. Nothing takes Him by surprise.

Expressing gratitude for God's past and present provision is one of the most effective ways we cultivate trust in his future provision. Our clients, sensing the peace that results the confidence this gives us in God, are often encouraged as well.

That is the spirit behind the Baruch Ata. Praying it places one's attention on the true source of everything good. It is the Jewish equivalent of the Christian doxology: *Praise God from whom all blessings flow.*

We need prayers like these because we are inclined to forget our source. We can easily think, "I have become wealthy (or wise) by my own hand."

The book of Proverbs warns us against relying on ourselves in this way. It says that we must acknowledge God in all of our ways. If we do, the passage promises, God will direct our path.

It is natural, even healthy, to exude a reasonable level of confidence in our training and experience. Every accountant knows, however, that economic forces can take unanticipated turns. Some seasons are so intense that neither our training nor experience seem adequate. The resulting frustration and fatigue may lead us to make costly mistakes instead of seeking God for wisdom, courage, and strength.

Acknowledging God means, among other things, remaining aware of God's presence.

The medieval monk called Brother Lawrence was disappointed when his abbot assigned him cooking and cleaning duties instead of sending him out to preach. To avoid bitterness, he began reminding himself several times a day, "The Lord is here."

Soon, people began coming to his kitchen because they sensed the presence of God there. After a while, even the crowned heads of Europe made their way to sit and watch a simple monk cook and wash dishes.

For accountants as for anyone else, this is where prayer begins: with gratitude and awareness that our true source of provision and guidance cares about us. When we remain aware of God's presence, we lose any doubt that He will give us the guidance, integrity, and patience we need to carry out the work we do on behalf of others.

Bless you, Lord God, King of the universe, who brings forth bread from the earth.

Gratitude opens our hearts. Ingratitude closes our hearts. Open hearts discover new ways forward. Closed hearts fail to see novel solutions.

Unfortunately, most of us are inclined to ingratitude. After obsessing for years over some object or role in the world, how quickly, once we acquire it, we tend to dismiss its significance! If we're not careful, life becomes a matter of filling our shelves with trophies while we keep pursuing more distant dreams. Setbacks, even insignificant ones, become unbearable grievances. We probe our disappointments like we would an infected tooth, fascinated by the pain and discomfort.

Gratitude cures that kind of infection.

One of the more interesting people I have met in life was a well-known Black pastor called Bishop Ralph Houston. For most of his adult life, he pastored a large church in Los Angeles. One example of his influence in that city is that Mayor Bradley once asked him to head the delegation civic leaders to welcome Pope John Paul II at the airport. Bishop Houston was fiercely dedicated to building relationships among people of different races. So, his sphere of influence continued to expand through the decades.

As he aged, however, his health began to decline. Ultimately, he moved into a retirement facility in Murfreesboro,

Tennessee. Unable those last couple of years to attend to his personal care, this intelligent and respected man watched as his once large platform shrunk to that little room at the care center. His once-booming voice, known for its authority, faded to a mere whisper.

How did he cope?

Bishop Houston said that he had decided to see each change of life as "a new assignment." In his last years, he spent most days constantly reviewing a sheet of paper full of prayer requests from his nurses, his fellow residents, and the visitors. Confined to the bed, his lips kept moving as he quietly read each name on the sheet to God.

The last words anyone heard him say was, "Thank you, Lord."

Gratitude transforms life. Baruch Ata.

PRAYER:

Blessed are You, Lord God, King of the universe.

In infinite wisdom, you have given me life and sustained me. You have showered me with countless blessings and continually guided my steps.

Thank you for your boundless grace and lovingkindness. Thank you for the gift of each new day. Thank you for the beauty of creation and for providing all our needs. Thank you for family, friends, and wholesome acquaintances.

Teach me, O Lord, to recognize Your hand in all things, to see Your blessings even in the midst of challenges.

Grant me the grace to be grateful for small things, to appreciate ordinary moments, and to find joy in the simple pleasures of life. May my heart be ever turned towards You, acknowledging Your gifts with humble thanks.

Amen.

REFLECTION:

_____
_____
_____
_____
_____
_____
_____
_____
_____
_____
_____
_____
_____
_____
_____
_____
_____
_____
_____
_____
_____
_____
_____
_____
_____
_____
_____
_____
_____
_____
_____
_____
_____

Wisdom

5

*Lord, those who place their trust in you shall not be confounded.
Teach me to discern your plan for my life and to trust you when
my life takes unanticipated or uncomfortable turns. Guide me as
I attempt to assist those who seek my counsel, that my words and
actions will be life-giving to them and consistent with your
purpose.*

What an honor that people trust us to untangle, organize, and manage their finances. Sometimes, our clients have more confidence in our abilities than we have in ourselves!

Naturally, we want our clients to trust our competence and integrity. However, this trust can create a business relationship in which our clients become vulnerable. In some cases, they may even become gullible.

Such trust can lead us to view ourselves as wiser or more competent than we are. That exposes our clients (and us) to embarrassment and loss. It is proper for a professional person to project reasonable confidence in his or her experience and ability. However, it is also important that we remain aware of our limitations.

Healthy humility emerges from an awareness of our mortality. Our gifts and goods—indeed, life itself—are temporary. Our resources, tangible and intangible, are limited. What we know, we know only in part. Our motives are mixed. Our intelligence, health, and age limit us.

Ultimately, we die.

Thomas à Kempis wrote, "Think now and often on the hour of your death and on what state you wish to be found on that hour. Then, live that way today."

Past generations realized that a keen awareness of morality, far from being morbid, was the ground of wisdom. Wisdom, in turn, was what turned knowledge into action and character.

The apostle James said that when we lack wisdom, we can request it from God. This is a prayer God always answers, James said. While we may not always appreciate the way wisdom comes, if we desire it, we will find it.

Proverbs depicts wisdom as an elegant lady. She invites humanity to a great banquet. As we listen, a harlot named Folly urges us to stop taking life so seriously. The writer of Proverbs —traditionally believed to be Solomon—had experienced both folly and wisdom. So, he pleads for us to keep following Lady Wisdom.

To do that, he says we must stop leaning on our own understanding. We must instead acknowledge God in all our ways. If we do, the Lord will direct our paths.

Wisdom, in other words, emerges from humility. It comes to those aware that they are ignorant of many things. Praying for wisdom implies that we need it. Such awareness is already a form of wisdom. It means we can set aside our prejudices and egos to honestly evaluate whatever data, persons, and situations we face. We will not rush recklessly ahead, certain we know all there is to know.

Prayer for wisdom softens our hearts to new information and any insight that God may impress upon us. We discern the way forward until we sense the moment is right for action.

Along with competence and integrity, wisdom is a means through which God advances good in the world through those who serve Him.

In the Old Testament, Joseph suffered great hardships because his brothers sold him into slavery. He might have sunk into bitterness and despair.

Instead, he offered wise counsel to those who oppressed him, gaining favor and influence. Ultimately, he was instrumental in saving thousands of lives, including those of his own household.

Wisdom is a gift available to all. It is an indispensable one for those who manage the resources of others.

PRAYER:

Dear Lord,

As Solomon pleased you because he prayed for wisdom rather than for influence or wealth, grant me also the desire to grow in wisdom and knowledge, that I may be transformed by the renewing of my mind. In Jesus's name.

Amen

REFLECTION:

_____

_____

_____

_____

Integrity

6

Who may dwell in your sacred tent, and who may live on your holy mountain? It is the one whose hands are pure and whose heart is clean.

Psalm 15

I ntegrity is a special kind of wholeness—it describes a person whose values, words, actions, attitudes, and competencies align. Such a person says what he means and means what he says. He knows what he believes and acts accordingly.

An accountant with integrity has basic computation skills, for example. He has a reasonable grasp of laws related to taxes, investments, interest rates, and so forth. He has any credentials required by law kept up to date. He keeps his commitments. He balances reasonable caution with courage. The competence expected of one who manages another's goods aligns with the ethical and legal parameters set by the community.

An accountant possessing integrity, in other words, is what the clients assume him or her to be.

An accountant with integrity invests the time required to

maintain his or her knowledge base. He realizes that laws and economic seasons change. Since accounting procedures change as well, he is a lifelong learner.

There are many reasons a client seeks the services of an accountant or some other financial consultant. Perhaps, the client lacks the financial worker's skill and experience. It may be that the client wants to focus on other things. In either case, the client should be able to assume that the financial worker is credentialed, keeps his knowledge and skills current, and knows how to create and interpret a spreadsheet.

Few clients ask for proof that a financial worker has personal and professional integrity; most of them assume this is the case. It is therefore the worker's responsibility to remain trustworthy of that confidence.

As in all professions, accountants will face situations that require knowledge the accountant lacks. Few clients will be upset by this. They may even find it reassuring when their accountant refuses to act on partial knowledge and reveals their need to seek more information. The client realizes that his or her accountant does not claim more knowledge than they possess.

Such occasions become opportunities for spiritual and professional growth. Navigating them well deepens the financial worker's competence and wisdom. Experience and integrity combine to extend one's capacity and reliability.

The ground of a steward's integrity is this: we deal with another person's (or group's) finances. The goods we steward are not ours. We are not therefore entitled to the personal use of any object, information, or relationship we manage on behalf of another. We always remain aware of that as we serve our clients.

This is one feature of our profession that offers spiritual understanding. The Bible tells us that nothing we call our "own" is ours. All things everywhere are God's. We steward resources—whether they are legally ours or those of another—for a season. Knowing that all things belong to God cultivates a sense of stewardship rather than entitlement.

Integrity emerges from that very knowledge.

Jesus said that on the last day, God will evaluate how we have managed our resources, lives, and relationships. We want to hear God say, "Well done, good and *faithful* servant." We want to know on that day that we have had integrity.

Thomas Aquinas asked, "Who is a godly man?"

His answer?

A godly man is one who knowing the good thing to do, does that thing, day after day after day.

May God grant us the strength to maintain lives and careers known for their honesty and integrity.

PRAYER:

Heavenly Father,
Just as you are undivided within yourself, taking counsel within your own will, though without confusion of either person or purpose, teach me to reach toward that same unity of mind, soul, and strength that produces resolute and godly character. For Christ's sake.
Amen

REFLECTION:

_____

_____

_____

_____

_____

_____

Generosity

7

Do all the good you can,
By all the means you can,
In all the ways you can,
In all the places you can,
At all the times you can,
To all the people you can,
As long as ever you can.

John Wesley

The core belief of the Christian faith is that God, through Christ, brings healing to the diseased human soul and that receiving this gift requires only that we acknowledge our illness and accept God's unmerited favor.

Christianity, in other words, derives from trust in God's generosity. Some early Christians taught that creation itself overflowed from God's generous nature.

In some Jewish groups, a host will pour wine into a glass at Passover until it overflows, symbolizing divine generosity. The apostle John adds a Christian voice to this gesture, praying that his readers will in all things flourish, just as their soul flourishes.

The discipline of tithing was likewise meant to teach us that our source of sustenance is immaterial. God, who creates things from nothing, never runs out of resources. Tithing demonstrates our trust in that inexhaustible supply.

We need not fear that generosity will impoverish us. Wise giving is an investment that yields surprising and often unforeseen benefits.

Generosity helps us avoid envy.

Often, a client's finances exceed our own. It is easy to become envious and resentful, especially when we face financial challenges of our own. Cultivating a generosity of spirit enables us to resist comparing ourselves with others. Instead, we focus on the generosity of God toward us. We meditate on the joy that comes from generosity toward others.

Jesus once saw a widow contributing a few dollars to the upkeep of the temple. Others were making much larger contributions and letting everyone know it. Jesus said that the widow was giving more than the others. That was not true literally, of course. Jesus knew that her contribution was making little practical difference. The impact on her spiritual life, however, was great.

The widow, wanting to participate in the upkeep of God's house, gave as an act of devotion, unconcerned that her offering seemed insignificant. She gave because she was generous.

Jesus said that it was more blessed to give than to receive. While religious con artists have misused this passage to manipulate naive people, its truth remains. Nonmanipulative giving heals us of an undue preoccupation with money. That obsession can imprison the poor within a culture of poverty. It can also create indifference in those who are wealthy.

I was raised in an Appalachian community. Especially by today's standards, it was unbearably poor. For some reason though, I never embraced poverty as a self-image. I believe this was due to the generosity of the people who sponsored my education. When that opened doors to financial flourishing in my life, I knew that God wanted me to share those resources with others.

I had freely received. God should freely give.

Pastor Dan Scott told me about the mountain preacher in his youth—also in coal country—who would lead his congregation in a round while the offering was received. The lyrics of the round, which the congregants sang many times during each service, were:

> *"If you give unto the Lord, he will give you more*
> *to give."*

Many Black congregations in my youth sang something similar during the collection:

> *"We are sharing. We are sharing. Because the*
> *Lord's been good to me."*

In the book of Acts, an angel appeared to Peter. The angel's message was that Peter should share the gospel with a Roman centurion. Peter was understandably alarmed. The Roman army was an occupying force. Jews tried to avoid soldiers when they could. The angel assured him though that the centurion had touched God's heart. The man's generosity was known in heaven, and God is a debtor to no one.

PRAYER:

Heavenly Father,
The entire universe emerges from the generous overflowing of
yourself. Even when we had lost our way, you maintained your

generous ways toward us, by sending a Savior to deliver us from bondage and death.

Just as your generosity provides for our spiritual and material needs, help us to be tenderhearted and generous to our neighbors, not withholding anything that might provide for their good. For Christ's sake, who gave everything for us, we ask.

Amen

REFLECTION:

_____
_____
_____
_____
_____
_____
_____
_____
_____
_____
_____
_____
_____
_____
_____
_____
_____
_____
_____
_____
_____

Contentment

8

"I have learned in whatever situation I am to be content."

Philippians 4:11–12, ESV

Our sense of well-being depends on many things. We rarely have as much confidence in our judgment or find as much delight in our accomplishments when we are sick as when we are well, for example.

On the other hand, if we have just been awarded a large bonus for our work, we tend to overestimate our abilities. We may also exaggerate how well our lives are unfolding.

Much of our sense of well-being, in other words, depends more on our perceptions than on objective reality. A person who has an undiagnosed disease may feel great. A person with a cold may feel terrible. If these two people talk to one another, both will be mistaken about their own condition.

Most of our distress does not come from external events or physical setbacks. It comes from how we think. To a great extent, we determine our sense of well-being by how we explain things to ourselves.

When we are anxious about secondary matters, it is difficult to pray. We focus on our anxiety instead of trusting in God. Since effective prayer involves leading our hearts toward God, we must discover ways of dealing with anxieties.

Scripture urges us to be content with who we are and what we have. That doesn't mean we shouldn't be concerned about becoming better people, increasing our resources, or expanding our influence.

However, if we are anxious because we lack these things, acquiring them will probably not help much. The Bible insists that when we attempt to derive our sense of security from financial well-being, we often become more anxious rather than more content.

Spiritual contentment thus precedes success. We are nearly guaranteed disappointment when we assume that financial success alone will bring us the satisfaction we crave. For financial workers, this truth about life and joy relates to how we view money. It becomes either a tool or a god. That determines whether money is a blessing or a curse.

The writer of Hebrews (13:5) says, "Keep your life free from love of money, and be content with what you have, for he has said, 'I will never leave you nor forsake you.'"

In short, although financial well-being is desirable and wholesome, achieving it does not necessarily bring contentment.

Most of us know someone who lives in near obscurity, with perhaps few worldly goods, but who nonetheless seems content. Such people may not lack ambition. Like most people, they hoped to see the world, get a degree, or find a spouse. If they have realized these desires, they are grateful for them. It's just that these accomplishments seem not to be the source of their contentment. Furthermore, if they have failed to obtain some of these things, they are at peace, nonetheless.

A person like this has cultivated the attitude the prophet Habakkuk expresses.

> Though the fig tree should not blossom,
>> nor fruit be on the vines,
>> the produce of the olive fail
>> and the fields yield no food,
>> the flock be cut off from the fold
>> and there be no herd in the stalls,
>> yet I will rejoice in the LORD;
>> I will take joy in the God of my salvation.

Habakkuk 3:17–19, ESV

Every profession develops a culture and set of values—some align with spiritual life, while others do not. Sometimes, the culture that develops around financial work becomes spiritually harmful. The most seductive part of such a culture involves making an idol of money.

Jesus and the apostles spoke about that many times.

The apostle Paul, for example, said:

> Godliness with contentment is great gain, for we brought nothing into the world, and we cannot take anything out of the world. But if we have food and clothing, with these we will be content. But those who desire to be rich fall into temptation, into a snare, into many senseless and harmful desires that plunge people into ruin and destruction. For the love of money is a root of all kinds of evils. It is through this craving that some have wandered away from the faith and pierced themselves with many pangs.

1 Timothy 6:6–10, ESV

After decades of dealing with money, I still appreciate prosperity. However, my contentment comes from knowing and serving God.

Now, as I approach the end of life, I realize that I will soon leave my material resources to others. That doesn't concern me.

Although I would change several things about my life if I could, I work daily on placing those things in God's hands.

I am content.

PRAYER:

Heavenly Father,

Help me resist any sense of entitlement to any material thing or worldly honor that might blind me to the True Owner of all I am entrusted to manage.

Teach me instead to be grateful for life, love, and the resources that promote goodness, truth, and beauty in my life and in the lives of those I influence. Knowing that gratitude opens my soul to your Spirit, help me to begin and end each day with a thankful heart. Through Jesus Christ our Lord.

Amen

REFLECTION:

_____

_____

_____

_____

_____

_____

_____

_____

_____

Discernment

9

These were more fair-minded than those in Thessalonica, in that
they received the word with all readiness, and searched the
Scriptures daily to find out whether these things were so.

Acts 17:11, NKJV

Discernment is a kind of spiritual fumbling, akin to a
blind person using a cane to navigate his
surroundings.

Since none of us has enough wisdom or knowledge for
every situation we encounter, we must learn how to discern.

This is a gift that some people exercise naturally. It is also a
discipline that everyone can cultivate.

Feelings come and go, so we learn not to let them interfere
with clear thinking. However, discerning people don't ignore
their intuition either.

Likewise, training and experience are components of
discernment. However, they are not always sufficient for the
situations we face. As with feelings, we draw on our training
and experience while acknowledging their limitations.

As financial workers, we are sometimes asked to evaluate

investment opportunities. Exciting opportunities can easily overpower our better judgment. This happens to the most seasoned investor. It is especially seductive to those with less financial experience. Sometimes, we can offer a discerning perspective that saves the client pain and embarrassment. On the other hand, we may confirm that a given opportunity seems sound.

Discernment emerges from various aspects of our whole person. When we are walking in submission to the ways of God, information may come to us in ways we find difficult to explain. We can just know that "something doesn't feel right about this," or "I have looked at this as wisely as I can and feel at peace with it."

However, discernment does not end here. Intuition is an important part of discernment, but it is hardly infallible. We are mortals. Personal opinions, moods, and experiences influence our intuition. That is why we should critique our intuition. We examine the facts, consult with others, and, most of all, evaluate things in the light of Scripture.

In the end, discernment is a communal process.

In 1 Corinthians, the apostle Paul urges those with spiritual gifts to submit their gifts to a discerning body of believers. If someone in the church claims to have a revelation, the other members are to evaluate and judge it. The person giving the revelation is neither responsible for nor capable of evaluating its source or content by himself. In a discerning body, some will be more critical. Others will be more gullible. Some are more practical and rational. Others are more mystical and romantic. Some are friends. Some are not.

When a group evaluates something, everyone looks at it from several angles. They see its strong and weak points. They see its potential for good and potential for harm. Most of all, a discerning process exposes a matter to the light of scripture.

Loren Cunningham, founder of Youth With a Mission (YWAM), once told his community that God had called him to buy a ship and turn it into a floating hospital. God wanted YWAM to sail around the world, saving the lives of people living in poor nations.

Then, he added, "A ship is available! And it is a great deal!"

He was heartbroken when his community decided against making the purchase. However, he submitted to their judgment and didn't press further.

Later, someone donated a better ship to his cause. Wealthy donors stepped up to remodel and equip it.

Cunningham would tell the story when talking about discernment and say, "Sometimes, God is not using the community to reject our vision, but rather to help us wait on God's timing."

The apostle James said, "If anyone lacks wisdom, let him ask of the Lord, who gives it liberally."

Prayers for discernment are always answered.

PRAYER:

Heavenly Father,

Knowing that my understanding is limited and self-centered, grant me the ability to press beyond the surface appearance of things, so I may discern their source and end, and so choose wisely my reactions to those people, situations, and events I may encounter. Through Jesus Christ our Lord.

Amen

REFLECTION:

_____

_____

Intimacy

10

For we do not have a high priest who is unable to sympathize with our weaknesses.

Hebrews 4:15, ESV

In the ancient world, gods were autocratic beings. They did what they wanted when they wanted. Human beings had to adjust. The Hebrew understanding of God as an Almighty Being intimately concerned with humanity was shocking.

Jesus took the Hebrew idea even further. He called the Lord "the good shepherd who lays down his life for the sheep." (John 10:11)

He wept at his friend's tomb. He was angry about the temple's misuse of money.

Jesus revealed a God who responds intimately to others.

We learn from him how to be both capable and intimate.

Caring for the resources of others requires a "cool hand." We are trained to not overreact to challenging people or circumstances. No one wants to hear a pilot weep and wail about the storm the plane is passing through. In the same way, our clients are not comforted by our emotional reactions to the ups and downs of the stock market or other distressing situations.

Accountants and fund managers are not therapists or pastors. It is rarely appropriate—or even safe—for them to become involved in their clients' personal lives.

This professional demeanor, appropriate in most situations, can gradually become a cold and detached response to human suffering. We may find it difficult to recover our emotional self, even with family and friends. This nearly always affects our spiritual lives. Religion, in that case, becomes mere duty—if we retain it at all. Prayer, if it survives, becomes perfunctory.

Restoring appropriate intimacy in our relationship with God and others is thus an essential part of our spiritual journey. It often begins with brokenness. However competent we are, or believe ourselves to be, financial setbacks are always possible. Most of us will experience one or more of these in our careers.

Financial setbacks are difficult for everyone, but for those of us who care for the finances of others, they can be exceptionally devastating. For one thing, they challenge the core of our identity. We see ourselves as capable, competent financial managers. Perhaps, if we have enjoyed a long season of success, we even think of ourselves as financial wizards. A serious setback undermines this self-image and may even plunge us into a period of self-loathing.

In the movie Bruce Almighty, Bruce Nolan, played by Jim Carrey, decides he would do a better job than God at running the universe. So, God decides to allow him to show his stuff. After using God's power to get himself the best car and show off for people in a café, Bruce begins making all kinds of foolish decisions. He allows everyone to win the lottery, for example. Everyone wins $8.25. He ultimately makes a mess of things and pleads with God to take control.

It's a great analogy to what can happen when things are

going well. We make money for ourselves and our clients. We are praised. We compare ourselves well with others. We are a success.

A setback forces us to recalibrate. We suddenly need our friends and spouses. We want to talk about the meaning of life. We may not be able to suppress our grief or hold back our tears. Surprisingly, though we feel worse, our loved ones perceive us as having regained our true selves. We no longer go about like kings of the universe. We are human and approachable, intimate.

If we are fortunate, when the season changes again, and we are once more making competent decisions that evoke the gratitude and praise of others, we will hold on to the intimate life we regained during our time of trial. We will hold our self-image lightly, knowing it is only one facet of life. We have learned to weep with those who weep and rejoice with those who rejoice.

God becomes not only our Creator and Lord but also a friend who sticks closer than a brother.

PRAYER:

Heavenly Father,

The Lord Jesus told us that not one sparrow falls from the sky that you have not noticed, and that even the hairs on our heads are numbered. Grant me the courage to know others and to be known by them, as fully as is appropriate.

Deliver me from the isolation of a hardened heart and from any tendency to withdraw from those who are lonely or discouraged. Through Jesus Christ our Lord.

Amen

REFLECTION:

_____
_____
_____
_____
_____
_____
_____
_____
_____
_____
_____
_____
_____
_____
_____
_____
_____
_____
_____
_____
_____
_____
_____
_____
_____
_____
_____
_____
_____
_____
_____

Planning

11

Many things about tomorrow,
I don't seem to understand;
But I know who holds tomorrow,
and I know who holds my hand.

Ira Stanphill[1]

When I was a boy, people making plans for their future would add the phrase, "the Lord willing."

"We are going to build a new house next year," they would say. "The good Lord willing."

This saying came from the King James Version of the Bible, like many others we quoted. It was the only book many people had, and we heard its stories and phrases throughout the week.

This phrase originates from the apostle James's instructions to Christian merchants:

> Come now, you who say, 'Today or tomorrow we will go into such and such a town and spend a year there and trade and make a profit'—yet you do

not know what tomorrow will bring . . . Instead you ought to say, 'If the Lord wills, we will live and do this or that.'"

James 4:13-15, ESV

The idea here is that although believers should make plans —as Jesus himself taught—they do so with the awareness that, to quote John Steinbeck: "The best-laid plans of mice and men often go astray."

The writer of Ecclesiastes says much the same, claiming that "time and chance happen to them all." (Ecclesiastes 9:11)

In my experience, plans rarely unfold as we anticipate. Plans, therefore, should be reasonably flexible. That said, few people succeed in life unless they plan. Among the most important plans are our schedules and budgets. We use them to direct our time and finances toward our goals. An unexpected snowstorm or illness may overturn our schedule. An unexpected windfall or setback may affect our budget.

Fortunately, when we plan, the Lord, who knows the future, is with us. When we ask for guidance and wisdom as we work on our schedules and budgets, plans are more likely to fit the realities of the unknown future.

L. H. Hardwick was the founding pastor of Christ Church Nashville, where I worshiped for many years. He often told how he led the congregation to purchase property on the city's southern perimeter.

The location he had in mind was on a steep embankment. Some believed that showed poor judgment. Most of the congregants lived in a working-class neighborhood. In the following decades, many of them would be moving near, and even beyond, the property Hardwick wanted to buy. Of course that was in the distant future.

For Pastor Hardwick, the deciding moment came while

walking the hillside with his mother.

"Son, buy this property," she said. "The people will come."

At first, the church lost a few families. Even most of these returned after a couple of years. However, it also experienced dramatic new growth as younger families moved into the area. That growth increased over the following decades.

Pastor Hardwick was a planner. He would have been the first to say that taking calculated risks to keep his congregation relevant in a changing city seriously stretched his faith. His steps of faith were not foolhardy leaps into the dark, though. They were steps responsible people take when they believe God is guiding their plans.

PRAYER:

Heavenly Father,

Since we know in part and prophesy in part, it is not mine to know the vicissitudes of life that lie ahead. Help me to sense where you would have me go and what you have me do. Help me organize my time and focus my resources accordingly.

Amen

REFLECTION:

_____

_____

_____

_____

_____

_____

_____

_____

_____

Joy

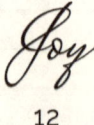

12

My life flows on in endless song;
Above earth's lamentation,
I catch the sweet, tho' far-off hymn
That hails a new creation;
Thro' all the tumult and the strife
I hear the music ringing;
It finds an echo in my soul—
How can I keep from singing?

What tho' my joys and comforts die?
The Lord my Savior liveth;
What tho' the darkness gather round;
Songs in the night he giveth.

No storm can shake my inmost calm
While to that refuge clinging;
Since Christ is Lord of heaven and earth
How can I keep from singing?

Traditional Quaker Hymn

Emma Thompson's performance in *Sense and Sensibility* (1995) is one of the most powerful scenes in cinematic history.

Thompson plays the part of Elinor Dashwood, one of three sisters who, following the death of their father, live with their mother in financially challenging circumstances.

Elinor is responsible and dutiful. She works to keep things intact as her younger sisters grow into adulthood. However, she is in love with a clergyman and hopes he will ultimately turn her way.

Alas, she learns that her clergyman, Rev. Edward Ferrars, will marry someone else. Her life settles into a dull and increasingly dead routine. The light seems to go out of her eyes.

One day, Rev. Ferrars comes to visit. Elinor fights to maintain her composure. When she asks about "Mrs. Ferrars," the clergyman seems confused.

Finally, he says, "Oh, my sister-in-law! She's fine! Thank you for asking."

"Then you ... you remain unmarried?" Elinor asks.

"Well, yes. That is why I have come by today," the clergyman replies.

The dam breaks. Elinor bursts into a wail of relief, unable to contain her overwhelming joy.

C. S. Lewis once remarked that the saints differ in everything except one: they are joyful.

Saints may not express joy like Elinor Dashwood, but they know what an unexpected blessing feels like. Even in stressful times, they have a "well of living water springing up into everlasting life." (John 4:14)

As we understand how much God loves us, how our eternity is secured, and how God's plan for us is unfolding, we experience what Scripture calls "joy unspeakable."

The Orthodox writer Alexander Schmemann, in his

memoirs, reflects on how religious people are often too suspicious of joy.

> *The source of false religion is the inability to rejoice, or, rather, the refusal of joy, whereas joy is absolutely essential because it is without any doubt the fruit of God's presence. One cannot know that God exists and not rejoice.*
>
> *The fear of sin does not save from sin. A feeling of guilt or moralism does not liberate from the world and its temptations. Joy is the foundation of freedom, where we are called to stand[1].*

This insight—that the fear of sin does not save us from sin—is priceless.

Satan tempts us to sin, and when we fall, he mocks us. The erosion of joy that results can become a "godly sorrow produces repentance." (2 Corinthians 7:10)

Unfortunately, it too often becomes a permanent part of our disposition. Even after sincere repentance and amendment of life, we can keep judging ourselves as unworthy of joy.

Schmemann claims this is a false path. "One cannot know that God exists and not rejoice," he says.

If God exists, and if, as the apostle Paul claims, God has justified us, then continued remorse can become a form of self-torture. This self-deprecating habit often masquerades as piety, yet it is actually a rejection of grace and life.

As the apostle Paul says, "Rejoice in the Lord always: and again I say, Rejoice." (Philippians 4:4)

How can we keep from singing?

PRAYER:

Heavenly Father,

Amid the sorrows and disappointments of life, you remain a well of inexhaustible joy. As the woman who stood by the well, craving something she could not name, so do I also pray: Lord, give me this water that I may never thirst again.

For have you not said that with joy we shall draw water from the wells of salvation? For Christ's dear sake, fill me with that living water. Through Jesus Christ our Lord.

Amen

REFLECTION:

_____
_____
_____
_____
_____
_____
_____
_____
_____
_____
_____
_____
_____
_____
_____
_____
_____
_____
_____

Accountability

13

Almighty God, you are the righteous judge of all humanity. I shall one day stand before You and give an account for all I have done and for all I have left undone. Please help me to do my work in such a way, and in such a spirit, that I will be found blameless on that day. As Daniel, your faithful servant, moved the heart of a pagan king, help the quality of my life and work to move the hearts of those to whom I am accountable, and in this way, bring honor to Your name.

Claude Blankenship

Luke 17 tells the story of Jesus healing ten lepers who had beens. forced to leave their families. When Jesus healed them, they were overjoyed and ready to go home. First, however, Jesus insisted that they should submit to a physical examination.

People occasionally experience these same kinds of dramatic healings today. Our Lord modeled what we should do when that happens. We should have a medical examination. A genuine miracle stands up to scrutiny. Besides, after the examination, it's easier to share the good news with those inclined to be skeptical of miraculous healing.

The Lord's words to the lepers imply that we should submit ourselves to every legitimate form of accountability.

John the Baptist was reluctant when Jesus approached him about baptism. Why should he baptize "the Lamb of God who takes away the sins of the world"? (John 1:29)

Jesus insisted, though. He explained that for him, baptism was to "fulfill all righteousness." (Matthew 3:15)

In other words, by being baptized, Jesus meant to set an example for others. John the Baptist was "the authority" on baptism at that time. Therefore, Jesus, like all disciples, would submit himself to John, and to the rite of baptism.

Jesus was accountable.

Jesus had the same attitude toward the Roman government. He paid his taxes and told his disciples to do the same. That was astounding. Jews weren't happy about the Roman government.

Few people like being told what to do. We realize that, without government, communities fall into chaos. So, we don't want anarchy. At the same time, we believe we know how to do our job without the tons of rules and processes the government constantly creates—especially in our financial field.

Sometimes, oversight is not only inconvenient or incompetent, but scary.

In the Old Testament, Daniel was unjustly convicted by a corrupt government. He not only maintained faith in God but also remarkably showed respect toward the king who convicted him!

After Daniel was exonerated, the king's trust in Daniel deepened. He even made an official proclamation to honor Daniel's God.

The apostle Paul, himself a victim of governmental injustice, urged us to pray for those in authority and to submit ourselves to them.

As citizens of a democracy, we can work to get unreasonable laws overturned. As long as they are in force, however, we must submit to them. Only in the rare case where human law clearly violates God's law may we respectfully resist. Even then, we must be prepared to gracefully accept the consequences.

Government oversight of financial work is often burdensome. For one thing, laws constantly change, and we rarely know why. Nonetheless, we are responsible for knowing and submitting ourselves to those laws and regulations. If we do that, we have no reason for anxiety when we are audited or investigated. Indeed, such situations can reveal our character and values.

We are accountable, then, to our clients, our company, our community, the government, and our professional ethics. Most of all, we are accountable to the Righteous Judge of the Earth. He taught us to do justly, love mercy, and walk humbly.

To make ourselves accountable to these things is to accept the yoke of Christ and thus "learn of Him." (Matthew 11:29)

PRAYER:

Heavenly Father,

Grant me the grace to submit to all lawful authority and accountability that you have appointed to govern and restrain the moral faults to which I am prone.

Help me, especially in those times I become irritated by the flawed nature of those who govern and the imperfections of the systems they put in place. Help me, when possible, to improve these systems and, in all cases, to respect the boundaries You have set to restrain human waywardness. Through Jesus Christ our Lord,

Amen

REFLECTION:

_____
_____
_____
_____
_____
_____
_____
_____
_____
_____
_____
_____
_____
_____
_____
_____
_____
_____
_____
_____
_____
_____
_____
_____
_____
_____
_____
_____
_____
_____
_____
_____
_____
_____

Serenity

<blockquote>14</blockquote>

*Feelings come and feelings go, and they are deceiving. My
warrant is the Word of God; naught else is worth believing.
Though all my heart should feel condemned for want I have some
sweet token, I know One greater than my heart, whose word
cannot be broken. I will trust in God's unchanging word till soul
and body sever. The words of men will pass away, and God's
Word abides forever.*

Martin Luther

Commercial pilots experience challenging situations. Unpredictable weather, mechanical issues, and seriously ill passengers are always possibilities. We sympathize with the pilots. We just don't want to know how distressed they are until these crises are over. For example, it would not be helpful for a pilot to break down and weep while informing us of a mechanical issue!

A minister told a story years ago about a flight he was on from New Orleans to Birmingham. Before taking off, the pilot made an announcement.

"Ladies and Gentlemen, tonight's flight to Birmingham will

be brief. However, it's a stormy night with a lot of air traffic. We usually fly around these kinds of storms. Tonight, that will be impossible. So, we will be flying through the storm.

"We pilots are used to the kind of bumpy flight we will experience this evening. We know that this aircraft is built for much, much worse, and that the flight is entirely safe. It will not be comfortable for you, however. We will not be serving beverages. You will not be able to walk around.

"I assure you though, we will get you to Birmingham and to your families."

The bumps began soon after take-off. The plane began tossing this way and that. A few people became ill. Everyone was concerned, but no one talked much.

Every few minutes though, the pilot talked to the passengers.

"Hope you guys are doing ok back there. Once again, I remind you that this aircraft is built to withstand much more dangerous weather. We pilots are also trained for much worse. So, we are not concerned. We know that this is an entirely safe flight. We are right on schedule. Soon you will greet your loved ones in Birmingham."

Although the flight was uncomfortable, the serene pilot kept the passengers reassured. The plane landed safely in Birmingham.

Right on time.

Just as he promised.

Few of us have that pilot's serenity—at least in a storm. However, it is possible to cultivate it. The pilot knew his plane. He knew his level of training. He was in communication with the towers on the ground and other pilots. He was also experienced.

Perhaps this metaphor works best if we think of ourselves as passengers relaying the pilot's message to others. We tell the anxious, hard-of-hearing person beside us, "The pilot says there is nothing to worry about! We're right on schedule!"

That's what saints do: they repeat the pilot's words to their anxious fellow passengers. Like Isaiah, we have heard our Lord say, "Comfort ye, comfort ye, my people. Speak ye comfortably to Jerusalem, and cry unto her, that her warfare is accomplished, that her iniquity is pardoned." (Isaiah 40:1-2)

Amid the constant war, famine, and disease of the Middle Ages, Julian of Norwich said to her fellow Christians: "All shall be well, and all shall be well, and all manner of things shall be well."

We can even speak serenity into our own hearts. Psalm 131 says: "I have calmed and quieted my soul, like a weaned child with its mother; like a weaned child is my soul within me." (Psalm 131:2)

Like airplane pilots and saints, financial workers must remain calm during intense situations. Although we must tell our clients the truth, it's usually possible to do so in a way that calms rather than exacerbates the situation. Besides, solutions often come easier when we do not panic.

Sometimes, we need serenity to stay on the path toward recovery from our mistakes and addictions.

Alcoholics Anonymous and other recovery groups have adapted the first part of Reinhold Niebuhr's famous prayer.

"God, grant me the serenity to accept the things I cannot change; courage to change the things I can; and wisdom to know the difference."

Few know the rest of the well-known prayer, in which Niebuhr defines serenity from a biblical point of view.

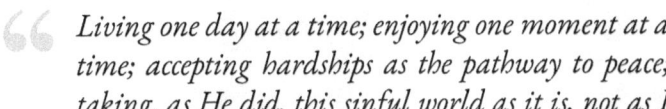 *Living one day at a time; enjoying one moment at a time; accepting hardships as the pathway to peace; taking, as He did, this sinful world as it is, not as I*

would have it; trusting that He will make all things right, if I surrender to His will; so that I may be reasonably happy in this life and supremely happy with Him forever in the next.

As those recovering from addiction know all too well, some hardships require us to recognize our powerlessness. This is not a denial of personal responsibility. It is an expression of our mortality and need for God. It is the embrace of the process (and the pace) that moves us through the storm and on to home.

Recognizing that we are eternal creatures helps us understand that setbacks are rarely catastrophic. As the Scriptures assure us: "God makes all things beautiful in his time."

There are things we cannot change. We must accept them.

There are things we can change. We must address them.

We need wisdom to know the difference.

Serenity is trust in our Pilot, who says to us continually, "Be not afraid."

PRAYER:

God,

Grant me the serenity to accept the things I cannot change; courage to change the things I can; and wisdom to know the difference.

Living one day at a time; enjoying one moment at a time; accepting hardships as the pathway to peace; taking, as he did, this sinful world as it is, not as I would have it; trusting that he will make all things right, if I surrender to his will; so that I may be reasonably happy in this life and supremely happy with him forever in the next.

Amen

REFLECTION:

_____
_____
_____
_____
_____
_____
_____
_____
_____
_____
_____
_____
_____
_____
_____
_____
_____
_____
_____
_____
_____
_____
_____
_____
_____
_____
_____
_____

Patience

15

Do not overly despair when people disappoint you. For even if all your efforts, your arguments, and your persuasion fail, then there is another remedy left that remedy is frequently found effectual with no other method avails; the method of prayer.

John Wesley, *When All Else Fails, God Does Not*

J ohn Wesley once preached a sermon called, *When All Else Fails, God Does Not*. Here are a few more quotes:

" *Therefore, now at least, ask, and it shall be given unto you. Ask, that you thoroughly experience, and perfectly practice, the whole of that religion that our Lord has so beautifully described. If you ask, it shall then be given to you, to be holy, both in heart and conversation.*

And another:

> *Seek in the way he has ordained, by searching the Scriptures, and hearing his words; by meditating, fasting, and partaking of the Supper of the Lord, you shall find the pearl of great price. You will find that faith that overcomes the world. You will find that peace that the world cannot give. That love is your inheritance. Knock. Continue in prayer and every other way of the Lord. Do not grow weary or faint in your mind. Press on to the mark. Take no denial; do not let him not go until He blesses you.*

And finally:

> *The door of mercy, holiness, and heaven will open to you.*

Among the many King James phrases that sound strange to contemporary ears is the term "long-suffering."

Most contemporary versions replace the terms with the word "patience." That is a reasonable translation. However, the contemporary word is less spiritually descriptive. Long-suffering implies a kind of tempered character produced by enduring stress and hardship over time.

It is difficult to accept that some of our deepest longings may remain unfulfilled in this life. Some of us will not become wealthy. Some will not experience romantic love. Some will not have children. Some will not achieve notoriety in their chosen field. Some will struggle with physical abnormalities. Some will be falsely accused, even convicted, of things they did not do. Some will experience heartbreaking loss of various kinds.

A life of faith does not spare us from such disappointments.

At times, even blessings can become hardships. How many people born with exceptionally good looks fail to cultivate knowledge and skill because early success came so easily? Some find it unbearable when age erodes their physical beauty. Talent can promise fame, only to disappoint when trends shift.

When we are young, we assume that we will overcome all our difficulties. If they instead become permanent features of our lives, we may fall into despair. Life, in that case, can become an embittered endurance of "things we cannot change."

One is reminded of old photographs of elderly couples, their faces frozen in silent resignation.

To be fair, people had to remain still in the early days of photography. The photographer thus probably recorded a moment that reveals more frustration with the photographer than with life. Still, it's a good metaphor. Sheer endurance can become chronic depression.

When the Bible talks about patience, or long-suffering, it's not attempting to characterize depression, despair, and resignation into virtues. What the Bible is talking about is a kind of spiritual alchemy that transforms challenges into character-building exercises. A person walking through such an exercise would probably welcome the removal of the challenge. However, he also has placed the matter in God's hands—most of the time.

Patience develops from learning to view current situations in the light of eternity. 2 Corinthians 4:17 tells us that our "light affliction" prepares us for an "eternal weight of glory." (2 Corinthians 4:17)

C. S. Lewis wrote one of his most famous essays on that verse, noting that the apostle Paul had reversed the way we tend to think: heavenly things as light and earthly, material things as possessing weight or substance. In *The Great Divorce*, Lewis depicts the newly deceased as ephemeral, wispy, and barely existent. They are not yet prepared for the more substantive, dense realities of Heaven.

Using Lewis's allegory of the apostle Paul's words, we can read the passage as saying something like, "The bursts of air that toss your flimsy soul this way and that are actually preparing you for a substantive existence to come—an existence you cannot imagine."

When we face challenging things, words like these can seem hollow, especially when spoken by someone whose life seems easier than ours. The one who wrote those words however, faced every sort of imaginable difficulty. In fact, he wrote them while was waiting for a court-ordered beheading.

For Paul, patience was not mere endurance. It was endurance fortified by faith in the God who had called him. That is what the King James version means by "long-suffering."

PRAYER:

Almighty God,

You order all things in your perfect wisdom: Grant me the patience and steadfast trust in your divine timing, that I may find peace in the knowledge that both the delay and the fulfillment of my hopes are expressions of your sovereign will.

Teach me to rest in the peace that surpasses all understanding, confident that in the waiting, as well as in the answer to my prayer, you are shaping my soul according to your own purpose. Through Jesus Christ the Lord, and through the work of the Holy Spirit.

Amen

REFLECTION:

_____

_____

_____

Guidance

16

*The steps of a man are established by the Lord, when he delights
in his way; though he fall, he shall not be cast headlong, for the
Lord upholds his hand.*

Psalm 37: 23-24, ESV

E velyn Underhill once compared the soul to a telegraph
station.

The soul, she said, continually receives messages
from outside itself. Sometimes, though, there is static. The
receiving instrument may not function as it should. The telegraph operator's attention can lag. Although the transmitted
information is clear and accurate, the soul often misinterprets
it.

It is a metaphor from a bygone era, yet I find it helpful.

The Bible is an accurate carrier of God's Word. The Holy
Spirit always transmits truthfully. The Body of Christ, in every
century and every human culture in which it has found a home,
proclaims God's will and purpose through the preached word,
corporate worship, and service to humanity. Nature itself
reflects God's character and design.

We are both surrounded and permeated by spiritual information.

Alas, our receiver is flawed.

That is why we pray for clarity, study the Scriptures, and seek discerning counsel from others.

I have a personal example of how this works.

A few months after I had started a new company, I had a strong and persistent urge to do something strange. I was behind our house getting something from the shed when I suddenly experienced an eerie sensation. It was not at all unpleasant, just out of the ordinary.

I turned my attention toward what this might mean. Words began forming in my head: *join YWAM.*

Youth With a Mission (YWAM) is an international Christian missionary organization. Its members raise financial support as they serve around the world. So, this impression seemed preposterous. Joining YWAM would involve raising money to support our entire family because most of my children still lived at home. Besides, I was responsible for the new company we had started. My business partner was depending on me.

There were multiple reasons for not acting on this persistent impression.

I began to pray for wisdom. I needed to understand whether the impression came from God. If it did, I needed to know how and when to respond.

In the next few weeks, I sought wise counsel. I shared what I was sensing with my business partner. I did everything I knew to judge whether this impression was divine guidance or an unwise diversion from my personal and corporate responsibilities.

To my surprise, the many pieces of my discernment process quickly aligned. My business partner suggested ways to organize my time. That meant I would not be abandoning our new company. An unlikely and unsolicited donor decided to underwrite us for a year of ministry. YWAM found a place of service for us.

It all came together.

In the years that followed, our family experienced serving God and others around the world. Meanwhile, our company prospered. In fact, I had a new vision for the company!

Most of all, I had deeper faith that divine guidance is always available.

It's unwise to act rashly on our impressions. As Underhill said, the "telegraph receiver" makes mistakes interpreting all the dots and dashes. Even the strongest impression calls for prayer, meditation on Scripture, and counsel from others.

A discerning process should not include merely those inclined to agree with us. I expected my business partner to disagree about deviating from our business plan. Nonetheless, I submitted to what I expected to be reasonable pushback from him. A man I consulted because I thought he would offer a cautious point of view, became our major donor.

The ultimate source of guidance for Christians is the Bible, a standard affirmed by the apostle Peter. After recounting his experience on the Mount of Transfiguration, he said that the Holy Scripture was "a more sure word of prophecy." (2 Peter 1:19) That's quite a statement from a man who had personally seen Jesus, Moses, and Elijah!

Many Jewish scholars teach that attentive Bible reading is a form of prayer.

What God has to say to us is more informative than what we say to God. Prayer, like all conversation, involves listening and well as talking.

In the New Testament, corporate prayer usually revolves around a Psalm. Corporate prayers used in worship—such as those in Protestant and Catholic prayer books—are often para-phrased Scripture passages.

Private prayer too can draw on this practice. We can use a Bible passage to express what we say to God. I have often received divine guidance this way.

John Cassian, a fourth-century missionary to France, said that each morning he would read Scripture until a word or phrase pierced his heart—then he would stop reading.

"That was my manna for the day," he said.

As he recalled the passage throughout the day, it shed light on the decisions he faced.

God is always speaking. Like young Samuel in the Old Testament, we must learn to say, "Speak, Lord, for your servant hears." (1 Samuel 3:9-10)

PRAYER:

Almighty God,

You order all things in your perfect wisdom: Grant me patience and steadfast trust in your divine timing, that I may find peace in the knowledge that both the delay and the fulfillment of my hopes are expressions of your sovereign will.

Teach me to rest in the peace that surpasses all understanding, confident that in the waiting, as well as in the answer to my prayer, you are shaping my soul according to your own purpose. Through Jesus Christ the Lord, and through the work of the Holy Spirit.

Amen

REFLECTION:

_____

_____

Presumptuousness

17

Have mercy on me, O God, according to your steadfast love;
according to your abundant mercy blot out my transgressions.
Wash me thoroughly from my iniquity, and cleanse me from
my sin!

Psalm 51:1–2, ESV

As an 84-year-old accountant, I have watched many people, including myself, wrestle with temptation.

When we face strong temptation, we sometimes reassure ourselves, thinking that God will forgive us if we give in. "Mercy triumphs over justice," we say. Imagine that! We plot about taking advantage of God's goodness by intentionally choosing to do something wrong.

The Bible calls this "high-handed," or presumptuous sin. It involves walking into wrongdoing with our eyes open. Deciding to sin, and even planning how to do it, is different than getting caught off-guard by circumstances. It often leads to serious consequences.

Psalm 19 teaches us to pray: "Keep back thy servant also from presumptuous sins; let them not have dominion over me:

then shall I be upright, and I shall be innocent from the great transgression." (Psalm 19:13)

We want to be free of all sin, but according to this prayer, presumptuous sin is especially disastrous.

King David wrote the 51st Psalm after the prophet Nathan confronted him over his presumptuous sin.

David had ordered the commander of the army, Joab, to place Uriah, in a situation in which he would be killed in battle. David had been sleeping with Uriah's wife, Bathsheba. Since Uriah was an officer in the army, it was easy to plan a clever coverup.

With Bathsheba pregnant with David's child, he assumed that Uriah's death would conceal his adultery. However, the Lord sent Nathan the prophet to tell David—and, by extension, us—that presumptuous sin has serious consequences.

In the confrontation with the king, the prophet told a story.

Two men lived in a certain city, one rich and the other poor. The rich man had a large flock of sheep. The poor man had merely one small ewe. The poor man had raised this lamb with his children. The lamb drank from his cup and slept in his arms. It was more like a child than an animal to the poor family.

In time, the rich man needed to feed a guest from another town. He could not bring himself to slaughter one of his sheep or cattle. Instead, he killed the poor man's lamb and fed it to his guest.

David was infuriated when he heard this.

"As the Lord lives, the man who did this deserves to die!" David said.

Then Nathan said to him, "You are that man!"

The Lord says:

> I anointed you king over Israel, and I delivered you out of the hand of Saul. And I gave you your

master's house and your master's wives into your arms and gave you the house of Israel and of Judah. And if this were too little, I would add to you as much more. Why have you despised the word of the Lord, to do what is evil in his sight? You have struck down Uriah the Hittite with the sword and have taken his wife to be your wife and have killed him with the sword of the Ammonites. Now therefore the sword shall never depart from your house, because you have despised me and have taken the wife of Uriah the Hittite to be your wife.

Behold, I will raise up evil against you out of your own house. And I will take your wives before your eyes and give them to your neighbor, and he shall lie with your wives in the sight of this sun.

For you did it secretly, but I will do this thing before all Israel and before the sun.'

2 Samuel 12:7–12, ESV

When David heard this, he said, "I have sinned against the Lord."

Nathan said, "The Lord also has put away your sin; you shall not die. Nevertheless, because by this deed you have utterly scorned the Lord, the child who is born to you shall die." (2 Samuel 12:13-14)

After a time, Bathsheba gave birth to a son. David pleaded with God to save the boy. He fasted, went home, and spent the night lying on the ground. The elders of his house stood beside him to get him up from the ground, but he was unwilling and would not eat anything with them. On the seventh day, the baby died.

David's servants were afraid to tell him the baby had died.

They said, "Behold, while the child was yet alive, we spoke to him, and he did not listen to us. How then can we say to him the child is dead? He may do himself some harm."

When David saw that his servants were whispering to each other, he guessed that the baby was dead. So, he asked his servants, "Is the child dead?"

"He is dead," they replied.

Then David got up from the ground. He washed, anointed himself, changed his clothes, went to the Lord's house, and worshiped. Then he went home and requested something to eat. So, they served him food, and he ate. His servants then asked him, "What is this thing that you have done? You fasted and wept for the child while he was alive; but when the child died, you arose and ate food."

He answered, "While the child was still alive, I fasted and wept, for I said, 'Who knows whether the Lord will be gracious to me, that the child may live?' But now he is dead. Why should I fast? Can I bring him back again? I shall go to him, but he will not return to me." (2 Samuel 12:7-23)

Though God forgives presumptuous sins when we repent, their consequences remain.

From personal experience and that of my friends and colleagues, I have learned to continually ask God for deliverance from temptation. Without God's help, we can do great damage in the world and inflict unimaginable sorrow on those we love.

PRAYER:

Almighty God,

Above all things, deliver me from any willful and presumptuous rebellion against how you want me to live. Help me not to presume upon Your forgiveness by persisting in what I know is wrong.

Instead, grant me the grace to seek healing for my wayward heart, that I may please You in all that I think, say, and do. For Christ's sake.

Amen

REFLECTION:

_____

_____

_____

_____

_____

_____

_____

_____

_____

_____

_____

_____

_____

_____

_____

_____

_____

_____

_____

_____

_____

_____

_____

Trust

18

"I have been young, and now am old, yet I have not seen the righteous forsaken or his children begging for bread."

Psalm 37:25, ESV

I wrote the first draft of this journal at my son's beach house. I often stopped to think and pray, meditating on the vast Atlantic Ocean.

I thought about how my Lord had created this ocean millions of years ago. All this time, he has been watching over it. I was joining Him by taking pleasure in His splendid world.

"Lord, everything you have made is good," I said.

One morning, while looking at the ocean, I began praying for a friend's father. He was 81 years old and in the hospital, recovering from open-heart surgery.

I thought, *Like me, he was once young. Now he and I have grown old. Throughout our lives, God has watched over us, noting our joys and sorrows. He has never forsaken us. We have never begged for food.*

Why would I fret about what I will eat or wear? God has always provided. He will always provide.

He is faithful.

In Deuteronomy 8, the Lord reminded His people of His past provisions:

> All the commandments which I command thee this day shall ye observe to do, that ye may live, and multiply, and go in and possess the land which the Lord sware unto your fathers.
>
> And thou shalt remember all the way which the Lord thy God led thee these forty years in the wilderness, to humble thee, and to prove thee, to know what was in thine heart, whether thou wouldest keep his commandments, or no.
>
> And he humbled thee, and suffered thee to hunger, and fed thee with manna, which thou knewest not, neither did thy fathers know; that he might make thee know that man doth not live by bread only, but by every word that proceedeth out of the mouth of the Lord doth man live.
>
> Thy raiment waxed not old upon thee, neither did thy foot swell, these forty years.
>
> Deuteronomy 8:1–4, KJV

God did not remind his people of his provision to seek praise but to assure them of his faithfulness and commitment to his promises.

It's an important lesson. We cannot pray with faith unless we are confident that God will fulfill his promises. We can be mistaken about how God acts in the world, but we must not doubt that whatever God does is good. He promised to save us. He promised to provide for our needs. He promised to guide us in the way we should go.

God is trustworthy to do these things.

As a child in our little Methodist church, we often sang Louisa Stead's hymn, "Tis So Sweet to Trust in Jesus."

> *Jesus, Jesus, how I trust Him*
> *How I've proved Him o'er and o'er*
> *Jesus, Jesus, precious Jesus*
> *Oh, for grace to trust Him more.*[1]

Hymns like this taught us the lesson God gave his people in Deuteronomy. They helped us take that lesson into our hearts and apply it to our everyday lives.

Over time, we learn that because God is trustworthy, His people must also strive for trustworthiness.

Financial workers must have a reputation for trustworthiness. After all, who wants to hire a deceptive accountant or funds manager? As children of God though, we want more than reputation. We want to *be* trustworthy.

George Washington often wrote in his journal about being trustworthy. He was concerned about living an upright life as a model for the people of his young country. After serving two terms, he stepped down from his position. No one wanted him to do that.

However, Washington was concerned that people would begin to make him a king. The type of democracy the founders had constructed had not been practiced before. Washington wanted to model what a democratically elected leader would look like.

Washington did two crucial things to shape the nation's future: he led the army to victory in the fight for independence and voluntarily limited his presidency to two terms.

For those who manage the wealth of others, trustworthiness is an important part of our work. For a Christian, it is vital to who we are.

Praying for trustworthiness is asking to reflect God's character, whose words and deeds are always true and faithful.

PRAYER:

Almighty God,

Teach me to trust in you and to become trustworthy for others. In those times when trust is hard, help me recall the many occasions when you have provided for my material and spiritual needs.

Help me to do the same for those I serve, that my actions may contribute to their stability and peace, encouraging their growth in you. In Christ's name.

Amen

REFLECTION:

_____

_____

_____

_____

_____

_____

_____

_____

_____

_____

_____

_____

_____

_____

_____

_____

Vision

19

For which of you, desiring to build a tower, does not first sit down and count the cost, whether he has enough to complete it?

Luke 14:28, ESV

Dan Scott, who helped me write this book, once lived in countries with extremely poor populations. After returning to the United States with his wife and two children, he found the financial realities of American life challenging. The idea of financial planning was particularly baffling.

An insurance agent helped him grasp the importance of financial planning.

"Imagine an old man living alone fifty years from now," the insurance man said. "That old man no longer works. He depends on the benevolence of a thoughtful young man."

"Both of these men are you," the salesman continued. "That old man eats and has a home because you consistently send a modest percentage of your income to him."

This vision of his future made a lasting impression. It

reframed financial responsibility as a spiritual practice, transforming a begrudging duty into an act of service.

Traditionally, people counted on their children to sustain them in their old age. Today, that is not considered virtuous. In a market economy like ours, we create incentives for an individual to care for himself. This is not the sort of "laying up treasures" Jesus warned against. It is a responsible practice based on economic realities.

In their 1996 book *The Millionaire Next Door*, Thomas J. Stanley and William D. Danko described a shocking discovery from their research. The largest group of retired Americans with at least a million dollars, were public school teachers!

These teachers had lived for decades within the means dictated by their low pay. However, they had also participated in the matching fund offerings from the schools where they taught. Many of them had been so disconnected from these investments that they had not realized how their regular, small investments had accumulated. They were stunned to learn that they were moderately wealthy.

Although the economy has changed since that book was written, the lesson remains. Even clients with modest incomes —especially clients with modest incomes—should plan for their future. As for our higher-end clients, especially ones who received an unexpected windfall early in life, many of them will be in trouble down the road because they fail to plan. That means that wealthier people also need a vision for the future.

The insurance salesman who had Dan imagine himself as an old man had hoped to make a sale. Most financial workers do not have that incentive, but they should still remind their clients —and themselves—to set aside some of today's resources for tomorrow.

Our consumer culture encourages us to spend on gadgets

and entertainment. We are urged even to go into debt for them. The working poor suffer the most from that culture.

It can seem cruel to encourage poor people to stay out of debt. The years can pass in which every day feels to a working-class person like endless, thankless toil. However, as one who has known poverty, I say with tears that that the way out of poverty begins by disentangling ourselves from consumerism. We cannot do that without a compelling vision for our future.

Psalm 126 says: "Those who sow in tears shall reap with shouts of joy!" (Psalm 126:5)

A missionary to an impoverished African country once told a story about how he had watched a tall, nearly naked man, walking to a shed behind his hut. The man unlocked the door and pulled out a large bag, which he carried to a dusty field. As he walked, he scattered its contents on the ground.

He was sowing seed.

A little boy was following behind the man, crying. As the missionary went closer, he saw that the man was also crying.

The missionary knew, then, that the man was sowing "precious seed," or "seed corn," into the dry soil. The man could have used this seed to make a few meals for himself and his hungry child.

Instead, the man had his eye on a potential future, on a time when that precious seed would become a year's worth of food. His vision was governing his present actions.

Some visions are grandiose, some are false, but some are godly intuitions about the future.

Without such visions, we perish.

PRAYER:

All-Seeing God,
Grant me courage and wisdom so that I may wisely send some

portion of my limited resources into the unknown future.

As you taught in the parable of the talents, help me to be neither foolhardy nor fearful, but to faithfully anticipate the coming harvest. Through Jesus Christ our Lord.

Amen

REFLECTION:

_____

_____

_____

_____

_____

_____

_____

_____

_____

_____

_____

_____

_____

_____

_____

_____

_____

_____

_____

_____

_____

_____

_____

_____

_____

_____

_____

_____

Darkness

20

Blessed is the man whose strength is in You, Whose heart is set on pilgrimage. As they pass through the Valley of Weeping, They make it a spring.

Psalm 84:5:6, NKJV

Over forty years ago, my sister Edith sent me a reflection by William M. Greathouse, the general superintendent of the Nazarene Church. It was about walking through seasons of spiritual silence.

"A sainted old holiness preacher once shared with me what he called his 'dry winter,'" Dr. Greathouse wrote.

"For months the only time he seemed to sense God's presence was while he preached. As soon as he stepped out of the pulpit though, he would return to his dry and thirsty land, where there was no water for his soul.

"Another active and exemplary church member confided in me that he too was walking in spiritual darkness, not from any known sin but rather from a strange withdrawal of God's presence.

"I know I have not broken with God," he said, "but my

prayers do not seem to get beyond the ceiling and the Bible no longer speaks to me."

John of the Cross called seasons like this *the dark night of the soul.*

We rarely know why we experience them, but they are common in the spiritual life.

Sometimes, darkness comes from unacknowledged sin. In that case, relief comes through repentance and making amends. Trusting in the mercy of God brings peace and so the darkness lifts. However, faithful people can walk through another kind of darkness. It involves a seeming loss of God's presence and a temptation to believe one has been on the wrong spiritual path.

Many of God's faithful servants have walked through this dark night. John the Baptist, for example, struggled with doubt while in prison, wondering if he had truly done God's will.

The Prophet Isaiah offers a word to those walking through the dark night:

> "Who among you fears the Lord and obeys the voice of his servant? Let him who walks in darkness and has no light trust in the name of the Lord and rely on his God."
>
> Isaiah 50:10, ESV

Job also experienced the dark night of the soul. Perplexed by his trials, suffering, disease—not to mention the false accusations of his friends—Job cried out in anguish.

> Behold, I go forward, but he is not there, and backward, but I do not perceive him; on the left hand when he is working, I do not behold him; he turns to the right hand, but I do not see him. But

he knows the way that I take; when he has tried me, I shall come out as gold.

Job 23:8–10, ESV

This is not the confession of a backslider. It is the cry of a faithful servant, longing for the comfort of God's presence. Job could not figure out why this darkness had overshadowed him.

> "My foot has held fast to his path; I have kept his way, and not turned to the side. I have not departed from the command of his lips; I have treasured the words of his mouth more than my necessary food."
>
> Job 23:3, 8-12, NASB

David wrote about the dark night in Psalm 22, the very prayer Jesus cried out on the cross when he felt forsaken by God.

> My God, My God, why hast thou forsaken me? Far from my deliverance are the words of my growing. Oh, my God, I cried by day, but Thou does not answer. And by night, but I have no rest.
>
> Psalm 22:1-2, NASB

When we go through a dark night, knowing we are in the company of great men and women of God comforts us. We take courage from their journey and believe that like them, "After we are tried, we shall come forth as gold."

PRAYER:

God of all Comfort,
Throughout history, many of your servants have walked

through seasons where their understanding and faith seemed inadequate.

If I too must walk through such a time, keep my heart fixed upon you, that I may move by faith toward the sure and certain hope you have promised to all who love you. Through Jesus Christ our Lord.

Amen

REFLECTION:

_____

_____

_____

_____

_____

_____

_____

_____

_____

_____

_____

_____

_____

_____

_____

_____

_____

_____

_____

_____

_____

_____

_____

_____

Prosperity

21

I know how to be brought low, and I know how to abound.

Philippians 4:11, ESV

Many years ago, a Presbyterian elder in Dan Scott's hometown saw him eating at a restaurant. Dan was surprised when the man asked if he could sit with him for lunch. Dan didn't know him well, though everyone in town respected him.

Dan had recently returned to the United States after living abroad. The elder wanted to say something about what might come next in Dan's life and ministry.

"The apostle Paul said that he had learned to be content in want and abounding," the elder said. "You have learned to be content in want. You have not learned to be content in abounding."

"Oh, I'm ready anytime to learn that—anytime," Dan said.

Laughing, the elder replied, "You might think so. However, wealth comes with responsibilities and challenges, especially for believers."

The elder prayed, then excused himself.

Dan was perplexed. It would be years before the elder's words made sense to him.

Most people who deal with finances go through both seasons of scarcity and abundance. In the rough times, we call on God. We get all the advice we can. We pay close attention to our spiritual lives. In times of abundance, however, it's easier to enjoy the ride. Deals seem easy to make. Money is easy to find. We sense the wind blowing through our hair. All is well!

The elder knew what he was talking about. He was a wealthy man. He had a reputation for walking uprightly before God. Nonetheless, he knew about the unique kinds of dangers that wealth and influence bring to one's spiritual life. He had not tried to avoid those dangers by denying his talent for making money, but he had remained leery.

He learned to be content in abounding.

Managing the finances of others provides knowledge, valuable connections, and opportunities for personal financial growth. We naturally want to put the "bad days" of scarcity behind us. What we don't want to do in the process though is forget the ways of the Lord. When God saw us through difficult times, we found his presence comforting. We focused on walking uprightly.

In some ways, reliance on God is easier in adversity and scarcity than in times of abundance.

In Deuteronomy 8, God instructs his people about remaining spiritually healthy in times of prosperity. They had only recently been enslaved. Now they were about to experience a different kind of life.

> For the Lord thy God bringeth thee into a good land, a land of brooks of water, of fountains and depths that spring out of valleys and hills;
> A land of wheat, and barley, and vines, and fig

trees, and pomegranates; a land of oil olive, and honey;

A land wherein thou shalt eat bread without scarceness, thou shalt not lack any thing in it; a land whose stones are iron, and out of whose hills thou mayest dig brass.

When thou hast eaten and art full, then thou shalt bless the Lord thy God for the good land which he hath given thee.

Beware that thou forget not the Lord thy God, in not keeping his commandments, and his judgments, and his statutes, which I command thee this day:

Lest when thou hast eaten and art full, and hast built goodly houses, and dwelt therein;

And when thy herds and thy flocks multiply, and thy silver and thy gold is multiplied, and all that thou hast is multiplied;

Then thine heart be lifted up, and thou forget the Lord thy God, which brought thee forth out of the land of Egypt, from the house of bondage.

Deuteronomy 8:7–14, KJV

An example from history can help us understand what God is saying.

John Wesley and his brothers were often ridiculed for preaching to coal miners and farmers. Because of the unruly, uncouth people they attracted, the Wesleys were not allowed to use church buildings. Although the Wesleys were highly educated, they ministered to people who rarely went to church.

In England and America at the time, that meant poor, working-class people.

By the time John Wesley became an old man, the Methodist

revival had lifted its participants out of poverty and ignorance. The children of domestic servants were attending college. Farmers' kids were leading successful businesses. Wesley wondered how the revival's social impact would shape the faith of future generations.

Wesley's observation about the social effects of faith over the generations is helpful. I have seen this same process at work in my own family. A life with God often leads us out of poverty, violence, and ignorance.

Whether in want or abundance, we always need God. That's what that Presbyterian elder meant in his words to Dan. It also concerned John Wesley.

When Presbyterians and Methodists agree about something, we need to take notice!

Prosperity is a blessing. It is also a challenge and responsibility. May we learn to treat it gratefully and wisely.

PRAYER:

Gracious Lord,

Only you know what I need to provide for my household and carry out the mission of life to which you have called me. When in your will you entrust me with talent, experience, influence, or material resources, help me to maintain an attitude of stewardship toward these things.

Help me to manage myself—and all the assets within my influence—in ways that glorify you and bless the world in your name. Through Jesus Christ our Lord.

Amen

REFLECTION:

Abandonment

22

My God, my God, why have you forsaken me? Why are you so far from saving me?

Psalm 22:1, ESV

Perhaps the most challenging thing I have faced in life has been dealing with real and imagined abandonment.

When family, friends, and colleagues leave, become emotionally cold, or betray us, it can feel as though the wound will never heal. Indeed, some emotional wounds never fully heal.

That's hard to accept.

We live in a nation of relative prosperity. Even the poorest rarely go hungry. Most of us are shielded from the elements. We have access to some level of medical care. We have come to think of this level of material security as normal. As a result, many of us have turned our attention toward meeting our felt needs, especially emotional and relational ones.

Advertisers constantly try to sell programs and apps to address these felt needs.

Our high, perhaps unreasonable, expectations sometimes

result in acute suffering. Emotional and relational setbacks can feel catastrophic.

The Bible writers present a different picture of human relationships. For them, betrayals, changes in how others perceive us, and even the complete loss of relationships happen to everyone. Our only certain relationship is with the One who remains closer than a brother.

God never leaves us. He never forsakes us.

People do.

When our loved ones are also in a relationship with God, we expect they will be willing to repair and restore damaged relationships. However, even among believers, we may encounter irreconcilable differences, shunning, and rejection.

In the 55th Psalm, David talks to God about his estrangement from another believer.

> For it was not an enemy that reproached me; then I could have borne it: neither was it he that hated me that did magnify himself against me; then I would have hid myself from him:
>
> But it was thou, a man mine equal, my guide, and mine acquaintance.
>
> We took sweet counsel together, and walked unto the house of God in company
>
> Psalm 55:12–14, KJV

One can feel David's suffering in this prayer, and if they have experienced something similar, they may find consolation in having words to express their own pain.

Dan Scott once told me about a group of people who had become antagonistic toward him. While walking through the woods with a friend, he confessed that he had developed hatred toward these people.

Hearing this, his friend asked, "So, would you like God to send these people to hell?"

"No! Of course not," Dan replied. "I don't want anyone to go to hell."

"Then you do not hate them," the friend replied. "You are just hurt."

The friend suggested that Dan pray each morning for these people. Dan agreed and began calling their names before God, asking the Lord to bless them.

After a few weeks, the deep hurt he had confessed to his friend had subsided. He realized that human beings often misunderstand one another. Most of the wounds we inflict on and receive from friends are unintentional. Knowing this, we release our friends and loved ones—including those from whom we are estranged—to God's care.

We'll understand it better, by and by, as the old song says.

Releasing bitterness opens our hearts to healing and prepares us to take joy and strength from the relationships that remain ours to cherish.

Sometimes people have abandoned us. Sometimes, our experience of abandonment comes from our insecurities. Jesus, in agony and alone, felt abandoned by God.

Three days later, the resurrection changed the universe.

Time has a way of revealing the truth. Meanwhile, we find comfort in releasing those who have hurt us into the hands of God.

PRAYER:

Almighty God,
You are the One who makes me strong. I come to you as I am,
with my sins and weaknesses. I confess my many sins and ask you

to remove them from me as far as the west is from the east. I rest in your presence, with my shortcomings in full view.

I am a jar of clay and so full of weakness. Therefore, I thank you for my insufficiency, for it has helped me depend on you. Help me, when I feel abandoned, to resist bitterness and resentment and to live in peace with all. In Jesus name.

Amen

REFLECTION:

_____

_____

_____

_____

_____

_____

_____

_____

_____

_____

_____

_____

_____

_____

_____

_____

_____

_____

_____

_____

_____

_____

Forgiveness

23

Oh, Lord, remember, not only the men and women of goodwill, but also those of ill will. But do not remember all the suffering they have inflicted on us; remember the fruits we have bought, thanks to the suffering—our comradeship, our loyalty, our humility, our courage, our generosity, the greatness of heart, which has grown out of all of this, and when they come to judgment, let all the fruits which we have borne be their forgiveness.

An unknown prisoner, Ravensbrück

This prayer was written by an unknown prisoner in Ravensbrück, a Nazi death camp. Rescuers found it beside the body of a dead child. It's nearly impossible to read without gasping, as it expresses an almost inhuman response to evil.

This prayer expresses the most shocking aspect of biblical spirituality: forgiveness is the heart of God's work.

As the apostle John wrote, "For God did not send his Son into the world to condemn the world, but to save the world through him." (John 3:17)

This implies that God forgives us even before we ask.

Although we are taught to ask God for forgiveness, God has already forgiven us. Knowing we have been forgiven leads us to forgive others.

This is why common prayer—that is, prayers we pray in common—so often deal with forgiveness. They teach us to express gratitude for God's forgiveness and for the grace to forgive others.

Although many people have no patience for poetry, I believe the reader will make an exception for John Donne great poem, *Wilt Thou forgive?*

The context for the poem is Donne's own life. He was a master of erotic verse who came to believe that his gift with words had led others to sin against their commitments to God and their spouse. After his conversion, he was the pastor of St. Paul's Cathedral, London, during the great plague. If fact, he died from the disease shortly after preaching a Sunday sermon.

After becoming a pastor, Donne wrote some of the most stirring spiritual poetry in the English language. His prayer of forgiveness may be his best. The first stanza confesses that although he had attempted to leave sin behind, it has been a life-long struggle.

Nor is that all.

In the second stanza, Donne confessed that although he had left a besetting sin behind for a decade or more, it had tripped him up again. He had even led others to sin in that same way. He longs for the assurance that God has forgiven him.

In the third stanza, Donne confesses his sin of unbelief. Although he tells others their sins are forgiven, he cannot accept forgiveness for himself. He prays for assurance that God will not forget him at the end of his life.

If God grants that request, he will ask for nothing else.

Wilt Thou Forgive?

by John Donne

Wilt thou forgive that sin where I begun,
Which was my sin, though it were done before?
Wilt thou forgive that sin, through which I run,
And do run still, though still I do deplore?
When thou hast done, thou hast not done,
For I have more.

Wilt thou forgive that sin which I have won
Others to sin, and made my sin their door?
Wilt thou forgive that sin which I did shun
A year or two, but wallow'd in, a score?
When thou hast done, thou hast not done,
For I have more.

I have a sin of fear, that when I have spun
My last thread, I shall perish on the shore;
But swear by thyself, that at my death thy Son
Shall shine as he shines now, and heretofore;
And, having done that, thou hast done;
I fear no more.[1]

Donne's request was granted. When his time came, he gathered his shroud around him, smiled, and breathed his last. Those around him said he died in peace and security. He died forgiven.

Prayers such as the one found at Ravensbrück and John Donne's verse guide us in shaping our own prayers of forgiveness.

Even if we have not been a pornographer like Donne, or a slave trader like John Newton, the composer of "Amazing Grace," we may wonder how God can forgive us.

Likewise, we probably have not experienced the level of harm from others that those persecuted by the Nazis faced. When we learn how individuals in these situations experienced God's forgiveness and extended it to others, we enter into the heart of God's work.

In our work as financial stewards, we may both do wrong and be wronged. This is the reality of living and working in a fallen world. With God's grace though, we can address our wrongdoing by asking God and other human beings to forgive us. We can also learn to accept God's forgiveness toward us.

PRAYER:

Almighty God,

Gracious Father, through the gift of repentance you offer inexhaustible pardon. For you have said that you do not hold our trespasses against us, neither do you mark iniquity.

Help us, then, to confidently ask for and receive your mercy, so that we may grow our capacity to forgive others, just as you have asked us to do. Through Jesus Christ our Lord.

Amen

REFLECTION:

_____
_____
_____
_____
_____
_____
_____
_____

FORGIVENESS

Timing

24

Teach me that prayer is not only a thing of times and seasons but is the outflow of life in you.

Teach me to draw near to you, Jesus, in prayer and the deep impression of my ignorance. I am a child and have a child liberty of access, and I have the spirit of Sonship and worship of truth.

Teach me, above all, blessed son of the father, how it is the of the father that gives confidence in prayer. And let the infiniteness of God's heart be my joy and my strength for a life of prayer and worship. [1]

Prayer is the Answer by E. M. Bounds, Andrew Murray, & John Wesley

Andrew Murray realized prayer was not merely "a thing of times and seasons." It was an outflow of relational life in God.

Scripture repeatedly reminds us that we are mortals. It also reminds us that God is not.

God is not subject to the vicissitudes of time and space. Our days, in contrast, unfold as Job says, "more swiftly than the weaver's shuttle." (Job 7:6)

Spiritual life is related to this difference between time and timelessness, between mortality and immortality. As God's children, we become immortal through God's kindness. In our present state, we are subject to the seasons of life.

Add the reference here Jesus told the woman at Jacob's well, "The time is coming and now is when they that worship me will worship in Spirit and truth." He meant that arguments about holy places had become irrelevant. He had inaugurated a new season.

The Bible speaks of such changes of seasons several times.

The Old Testament chronicler said the sons of Issachar "understood the times." (1 Chronicles 12:32)

The writer of Ecclesiastes said that the race was not to the swift nor the battle to the strong, but that "time and chance happen to them all." (Ecclesiastes 9:11)

Jesus said that he must "do the work of Him who sent me, for the hour is coming when no one can work." (John 9:4)

The apostle Paul, writing to Timothy, urges him to "come before winter." (2 Timothy 4:21)

Such passages encourage us to discern our current season of life.

As a man in my eighties, I have entered my final season.

When I envision myself, I don't feel much different than I was as a younger person. Others do look at me differently though. They see what I notice only occasionally, usually in a photograph. I am an older man. Some treat me with more respect because of my age, which I appreciate. A few people treat me more dismissively.

When we are young, we do not imagine ourselves as old. We see ahead of us years full of vitality and accomplishment. That season doesn't change abruptly. Year after year, month after month, day after day, little seems to change. Then, an event will alert us to the change of season. Perhaps it is when our children leave home. Or when we become grandparents. Or when our parents die. Or when someone younger than us becomes president. Such events can serve as a marker of passing time.

Having moved through all these changes, I have learned that each season has unique joys and challenges. Even older life has its advantages. When the elderly Jacob met Pharaoh, he was a far better person than the con artist he was as a young man. Young Jacob lived life to the hilt. He had little regard for others. Life changed him. He married. He had children. He faced great challenges. He had regrets.

Most of all, he had an encounter with God.

These events transformed Jacob. He gradually became the saintly sage who impressed Pharaoh. God even named the covenant nation after him, an honor not given even to Abraham.

God's work also moves and adjusts to seasons.

King Josiah was godly for tearing down the altars of other gods.

Daniel was godly for serving those who worshipped other gods.

Moses was godly for hanging a brass snake on a pole.

King Hezekiah was godly for destroying that brass snake.

Understanding and accepting our season of life, as we sense the changing season of the world around us, is an important part of successful living. Our great-grandparents would have been proud of becoming a skilled telegraph operator. Today, that skill is a strange hobby.

St. Brendan, the Irish missionary, drifted about in the North Atlantic, looking for a place to preach. If a contemporary pastor did that, we would question his mental health.

Like David, I can say that I was once young, and now I am

old. I know we can face all our changing seasons with confidence. After all, we serve the Alpha and Omega, the Beginning and the End.

PRAYER:

Lord of Time,
Teach me to observe and adjust to the season through which I move. Just as spring is for sowing, summer for growing, autumn for harvest, and winter for consuming, help me respond well to each season I encounter in the world and in my own life, that I may remain faithful and productive. In Christ's name.
Amen

REFLECTION:

_____
_____
_____
_____
_____
_____
_____
_____
_____
_____
_____
_____
_____
_____
_____
_____

Humility

25

Let not the wise man boast in his wisdom, let not the mighty man boast in his might, let not the rich man boast in his riches, but let him who boasts boast in this, that he understands and knows me, that I am the Lord who practices steadfast love, justice, and righteousness in the earth. For in these things I delight, declares the Lord.

Jeremiah 9:23–24, ESV

Most of us are familiar with the parable of the Pharisee and the Publican, a Roman tax collector.

Jesus said that both men had gone to the temple to pray. The Pharisee told the Almighty that he kept God's rules. He added that he was also grateful he had not sunk to the low estate of his fellow worshipper on the other side of the sanctuary.

Meanwhile, the publican beat his chest in sorrow. He told God that he was sorry for the life he had lived. "Have mercy on me, a sinner," he said.

Each man believed he had a clear vision of his own worth and spiritual state. However, Jesus reveals that both were mistaken. The grieving man left the sanctuary justified. The self-respecting man did not. That would have surprised them both.

God asks no man to grovel. Humility is not self-deprecation. Acknowledging our talents, experience, and resources is not necessarily an act of pride. Nor is self-abasement necessarily a sign of spiritual strength. Only God fully knows our hearts.

We do want to keep in mind that our resources, tangible or intangible, are given into our care for a season to manage. Sooner or later, that season comes to an end. The person we have become is all we take into eternity. That is why we do what we can to evaluate our present life as honestly as we can.

Long before the great psychologist Carl Jung talked about the shadow self, the prophet Jeremiah wrote, "The heart is deceitful above all things, and desperately wicked." He goes on to ask, "Who can know it?" (Jeremiah 17:9)

God interjects in the prophet's musings and says, "I, the Lord, search and examine the mind, I test the heart." (Jeremiah 17:10)

In other words, only God truly knows us.

Counselors often talk about "making the unconscious conscious," which is an important thing to do. In the end though, the depths of a person's soul is known only by God.

Robert Louis Stevenson's novel *The Strange Case of Dr. Jekyll and Mr. Hyde*, tells the story far better than any psychological text. A lawyer named Gabriel Utterson, investigating the crimes of a violent but elusive criminal named Edward Hyde, discovers that the thug and his kind friend, Dr. Jekyll are the same person.

Doctor Jekyll reveals that he had developed a technology to split the worst parts of himself, those parts he had repressed his entire life, from the well-meaning, respectable person he had led some to believe was his true self. Edward Hyde could express his darker side, leaving Dr. Jekyll to become ever more gentle and saintly.

It was an insightful work for those decades before contemporary psychology. The Bible had already told us this story, warning us that we do not fully know the depths of our own being.

Peter did not intend to deny the Lord.

Thomas did not intend to doubt the resurrection.

David did not mean to kill a man to cover up his affair.

The Pharisee did not know that his piety was false and unacceptable.

The publican did not know that his grief over his sinful life had touched God's heart.

I have known many powerful people. In their day, they were all impressive and formidable. However, as time passed, some of these apparent "good guys" turned and made a mess of things.

David learned to take comfort in God's knowledge of his deceitful heart.

He begins Psalm 139 in amazement, praying, perhaps in shame,

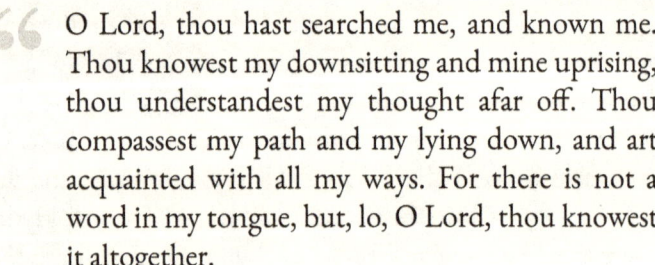

> O Lord, thou hast searched me, and known me.
> Thou knowest my downsitting and mine uprising,
> thou understandest my thought afar off. Thou
> compassest my path and my lying down, and art
> acquainted with all my ways. For there is not a
> word in my tongue, but, lo, O Lord, thou knowest
> it altogether.
>
> Psalm 139:1-4, KJV

He goes on to express how deep into the human soul God's sight extends.

> Whither shall I go from thy spirit? or whither shall I flee from thy presence? If I ascend up into heaven, thou art there: if I make my bed in hell, behold, thou art there. If I take the wings of the morning, and dwell in the uttermost parts of the sea; Even there shall thy hand lead me, and thy right hand shall hold me. If I say, Surely the darkness shall cover me; even the night shall be light about me. Yea, the darkness hideth not from thee; but the night shineth as the day: the darkness and the light are both alike to thee.

Psalm 139:7-12, KJV

David ends his prayer asking God to keep peering into his soul and to save him from further self-deception.

> Search me, O God. Know my heart. Try me and know my thoughts. See if there be any wicked way in me and lead me in the way everlasting.

Psalm 139:23-24, KJV

Authentic humility is not the pasted-on cultivated demeanor of Dr. Jekyll. Like the Pharisee in the temple, that personality was false. It may have expressed what the doctor wanted to be. However, inside that false persona was, as Jesus once said about some of the scribes, "full of dead men's bones." (Matthew 23:27)

I don't know if there is any better definition of humility than the quotation from Jeremiah at the beginning of this mediation: "Let him who boasts boast in this, that he understands and knows me." (Jeremiah 9:24)

That is my heart's cry, to glory in having found the one who knows me best and loved me most.

Thanks be to God!

PRAYER:

Heavenly Father,
Help me to think of myself as I ought, neither abasing myself in ways that cause me to lose awareness of Thy likeness in me, nor exalting myself in ways that dull my awareness of my many faults. Above all, teach me to honor others and seek their well-being. Through Jesus Christ our Lord.
Amen

REFLECTION:

_____
_____
_____
_____
_____
_____
_____
_____
_____
_____
_____
_____
_____
_____
_____
_____
_____
_____
_____

Worthiness

26

For I am the least of the apostles, unworthy to be called an apostle,
because I persecuted the church of God.

1 Corinthians 15:9, ESV

After the preceding meditation on humility, I thought I should say something about godly self-worth.

Even after years of effective service, can suddenly and inexplicably feel as though they have been fooling everyone. We call such attacks *imposter syndrome*, and it affects people in all professions.

This feeling is particularly common in spiritual life. Others hear our words and see our actions. We know about our fantasies, mood swings, envy, insecurities, and the other facets of our inner life. That is why the praise of others can sometimes feel undeserved.

If they only knew, we think.

While it's important not to think too highly of ourselves, it's also important to remind ourselves of the grace that both covers our imperfections and empowers us for service.

In his book, *The Heart of Revival*, Nicky Gumbel asks, "Who does God use?"

Gumbel then answers the question by reminding us that biblical figures were all flawed. David was unfaithful to his wife. Abraham had a problem with telling the truth. The young apostle Peter couldn't control his mouth. And so on.

We remember these characters differently because they became different people after responding to God's call. However, it is likely that they lived the rest of their lives suspecting they were not "out of the woods." The apostle Paul, for example, repeatedly refers to his sense of unworthiness due to his past.

There are several things we can do about imposter syndrome.

First, we can allow it to foster genuine humility. Scripture continually reminds us that we are mortals. An accident or illness can turn a strong person into a weak one overnight. The more a smart person learns the more he or she realizes how much more there is to know. Even the most morally upright person would not want others to be able to see their thoughts or dreams.

None of us are as intelligent, strong, or morally upright as we appear to others. It is healthy for us to remind ourselves of that.

Secondly, we can remind ourselves of past victories. When David was running away from Saul, a priest gave him Goliath's sword. The message was clear: you have already faced an enormous obstacle like the one you are facing now and prevailed. So, keep your head clear as you move through it.

Thirdly, we can resolve to be lifelong learners. Every new season of life brings new challenges. However, we face those challenges equipped by both our past experiences and our ability to learn new things. The saying that "you can't teach an old dog new tricks" is utterly false. If you need to learn something new for your work, or merely to satisfy your curiosity, accept the challenge!

Fourthly, we can ask for help. Few people think less of us when we admit our lack of knowledge or skill in certain areas. They are usually more than happy to share with us what they know because it allows them to shine.

Aging brings new reasons for self-doubt.

Our profession is much different today than it was when I began decades ago. The countless incremental changes in law, global finance, information technology, and workplace ethics present continual challenges. Sometimes, the knowledge of younger people in our field intimidates me. So does the ability of a specialist, someone who has learned a lot more than I have about some aspect of accounting.

We must remain aware that a sense of unworthiness comes to everyone at times. What makes it dangerous is when we try to cover it up by bullying others or manifesting some false bravado to keep them away from our perceived weakness. The truth is, most people we meet, like us, put on their best appearance, yet underneath, they too struggle with feelings of inadequacy.

When it comes to prayer and spiritual life, our sense of unworthiness can become overwhelming. From childhood, we hear about the characters of the Bible and the saints of history. We also notice the godly people in our early lives, usually older folk who seem serene and wise. We know we don't measure up to such people. Even after we get old, we know this!

The truth is, however, that those wise, serene people of our youth had their own struggles. We just didn't know about them. The same goes with the great saints of history, the best of whom said as much. We have often ignored that part of their stories because we like mythological heroes better than flawed ones.

Ultimately, our worth is grounded in this truth: we are made in God's image and likeness. Not only that, but Christ gave his life for us. He came looking for us because he loved us. He believes we are the prodigal son, the one lost sheep, and the pearl of great price.

When we enter the presence of God, we know we are there by invitation. We therefore belong.

We are worthy because we have been made worthy.

The apostle Paul must have felt inadequate because he struggled with some unknown weakness. He called it "his thorn in the flesh." In 1 Corinthians 12, he said that he asked God three times to deliver him from this affliction. God did not remove the thorn. Instead, he told Paul, "My grace is sufficient for you, for My strength is made perfect in weakness." (2 Corinthians 12:9)

Paul chose to view his weakness as a source of strength. "Therefore," he says, "I will acknowledge my infirmities, that the power of Christ may rest upon me."

If God has called us to serve others, lead a company, or manage finances, He will guide, equip, and sustain us.

We are never on our own, especially when we are trying to pray and thinking we are doing a poor job with it. Even then, we are trusting in the merits and help of the Lord who loves us.

PRAYER:

Lord,

I pray that you will strengthen my awareness of how you have equipped me for all you have called me to do. In those times when I feel inadequate, help me not to lose heart. For you have promised that you will never leave us nor forsake us.

Help me to remember that you have prepared me for the responsibilities that I now steward, so that with your help, I will not fail to accomplish all you intend for me to do. In Christ's name.

Amen

REFLECTION:

_____
_____
_____
_____
_____
_____
_____
_____
_____
_____
_____
_____
_____
_____
_____
_____
_____
_____
_____
_____
_____
_____
_____
_____
_____
_____

Formation

27

Blessed Lord, who caused all Holy Scriptures to be written for our learning: Grant us so to hear them, read, mark, learn, and inwardly digest them, that we may embrace and ever hold fast the blessed hope of everlasting life, which you have given us in our Savior Jesus Christ; who lives and reigns with you and the Holy Spirit, one God, for ever and ever. Amen.

Book of Common Prayer

Common prayers are ones we recite together, or "in common." *The Lord's Prayer* is, of course, the best known of these. *The Serenity Prayer*, often used in recovery groups, is another modern example.

During the early days of English Protestantism, Thomas Cranmer published a book containing a translation of the Psalms, the order of worship services, and important common prayers. This book has been one of the most widely published texts in the English language since that time.

Before the Protestant Reformation, common prayers were in Latin. While educated people understood their meaning, the general population memorized and recited them in church without comprehension.

In those days, before there was an official English translation of the Bible, Cranmer decided knowing the Psalms and the prayers most used in church would be a good beginning. The Book of Common Prayer ignited throughout England a desire for literacy. Following the publication of the King James Version of the Bible, this hunger intensified, sparking widespread literacy among English speakers in the decades that followed.

Great writers in English, such as Shakespeare and Milton crafted their works, and thus the English language itself, largely in the mold of The Book of Common Prayer and the English translation of Scripture. This pattern continued for hundreds of years. We see it even in the most important American documents and speeches, such as Lincoln's Second Inaugural Address. As late as John Kennedy's inaugural address, one hears the echoes of the Common Prayers and the King James Bible.

The common prayer for understanding the Bible expresses our awareness that scripture can be "inwardly digested." It's a powerful idea.

Most of us, most of the time, don't listen closely to the public reading of scripture. We may open our Bibles, or these days our phones, and read along. However, our minds don't automatically focus on the reading in such a way as to pull the passage into our inner being.

Even in personal devotions, it is common to rush through the words. Having done our devotional duty, we then go about our day.

Through common prayer, however, we remind ourselves that God caused all Scripture to be "written for our learning." (Romans 15:4)

To engage with God's purpose for giving us the scripture,

we ask that God help us to "hear, read, mark, learn, and inwardly digest" it. (*The Book of Common Prayer* 1662)

St. Augustine once compared the state of the unconverted human heart with the condition of the universe before creation. Our inner world is, without God, without form and void. Darkness is on the face of the deep. "The Spirit of God," Augustine said, begins the work of enlightenment by "hovering over the waters" of our hearts. Until we respond, our inner being is a godless universe. Our thoughts and emotions are chaotic and without focus.

Augustine goes on to say that God's creative Word not only formed the cosmos but can transform the chaos of our inner being. Because God has given to us the dignity of choice however, we must choose. We must ask for formation. When we do, God gives to us the transformative Word of the Gospel.

Psalm 119:130 says, "The entrance of Thy Word giveth light."

The Amplified Bible puts it this way: "The entrance and unfolding of your words give light; their unfolding gives understanding (discernment, and comprehension,) to the simple." (Psalm 119:130)

Inwardly digesting scripture, which includes memorization, meditation, quoting, and praying what we learn from the text, interiorizes God's will, character, and plan within the core of who we are. Just as the translation of the scripture transformed the culture of the English-speaking world, so can the inward digestion of scripture transform the hearts and minds of individuals.

Our prayer life is often the place where this inward formation begins to express itself. First, the desire to pray is a sign of that inward work. Prayer is a Christian discipline and should become a habit, like brushing our teeth or combing our hair.

However, little is accomplished if prayer is merely a discipline. When God is forming our hearts and minds, we ought to experience, at least occasionally, a draw toward prayer.

The blind Methodist preacher, William Walford, expresses this in his hymn, "Sweet Hour of Prayer."

> *Sweet hour of prayer! Sweet hour of prayer!*
> *That calls me from a world of care,*
> *and bids me at my father's throne*
> *make all my wants and wishes known.*
> *In seasons of distress and grief,*
> *my soul has often found relief,*
> *and oft escaped the tempers snare*
> *by thy return, sweet hour of prayer![1]*

The song describes a person for whom prayer is no longer a dead habit but the sincere longing of a soul in communion with God. In times of distress and grief—even when struggling with temptation—prayer arrives not as something imposed but as the natural expression of a heart formed by God's Word.

After decades of serving God, I can testify that although I am far from perfect, I have experienced what this hymn describes.

When struggling with some important issue in my personal or professional life, I have often discovered serenity and wisdom by taking a few minutes away from my anxiety to turn my face toward God and eternity. Usually, the answer came in the form of some passage of scripture, read or heard years before, when it had been "marked and inwardly digested."

PRAYER:

Lord,
Great God, who inspired the writing of Holy Scripture, give

me a hunger to know it, pray it, and live by it, that I may in turn become a living letter, known and read by all.

May I remain ever grateful for, and attentive to, that source of life and learning through which I am transformed and perfected. Through Jesus Christ our Lord.

Amen

REFLECTION:

_____

_____

_____

_____

_____

_____

_____

_____

_____

_____

_____

_____

_____

_____

_____

_____

_____

_____

_____

_____

_____

_____

_____

Intercession

28

So the men turned from there and went toward Sodom, but Abraham still stood before the Lord. Then Abraham drew near and said, "Will you indeed sweep away the righteous with the wicked?"

Genesis 18:22-23, ESV

One of the Old Testament's most powerful stories is Abraham pleading with God for the people of Sodom. It is in some ways a strange story. Although God was pleased with Abraham's intercession on behalf of the city, the destruction proceeded as planned.

What we are supposed to notice though is Abraham's willingness to argue even with God for the salvation of others.

"What if there are fifty righteous people in the city?" Abraham asked. "Will you sweep it away instead of sparing the place for the sake of fifty righteous people who are in it?"

As the bargaining continued, Abraham shouts in exasperation:

> "You could not possibly do such a thing: to kill the righteous with the wicked, treating the righteous and the wicked alike. You could not possibly do that! Will not the judge of the whole earth do what is right?"
>
> Genesis 18:22-25, ESV

Abraham steps to the very edge of propriety and reverence, frustrated and confused about how a righteous God could do something he thought unjust.

Even more astounding is God's response. God was pleased with Abraham, recognizing him as a man who understood both mercy and justice. From his small, human standpoint, God's intentions seemed unjust. Abraham was willing to risk his own life and standing with God to say so.

In the parable of the unjust judge, Jesus teaches a similar lesson. "We should pray for justice day and night," the Lord said, "giving God no rest." (Luke 18:7)

Jesus speaks as if God were an unjust judge who must be reminded to do what is right. It is an upsetting image.

The message is that God is never offended when we intercede for others, even if God knows that those for whom we pray will not change. Judging is God's business because only God has sufficient wisdom and knowledge to judge justly. Our business is to care deeply about those to whom we serve and to seek God's favor and blessing on their behalf.

As people who care for the resources of others, we often enter into the intimate details of their lives. We see things in them that others do not.

While we may or may not be offered an opportunity to speak into their spiritual lives, we must care deeply about that. We must care so deeply that we intercede for them before God.

PRAYER:

Most merciful God,
Just as you invited Abraham and Moses into your confidence,
and moved them to intercede for those who did not know you, help
me to join my feeble voice to the intercession of Christ and all those
who believe in Him, that the world may know and serve you.
Through Jesus Christ, our Lord.
Amen

REFLECTION:

_____
_____
_____
_____
_____
_____
_____
_____
_____
_____
_____
_____
_____
_____
_____
_____
_____
_____
_____
_____
_____

Legacy

29

O God, You have taught me from my youth;
And to this day I declare Your wondrous works.
Now also when I am old and gray-headed,
O God, do not forsake me,
Until I declare Your strength to this generation,
Your power to everyone who is to come.

Psalm 71:17-18, NKJV

As people age, they begin to think about how to pass their assets to their children. This is a natural, and even a godly concern.

The Bible says that "a good man leaves an inheritance to his children's children." (Proverbs 13:22)

At the same time, inherited wealth is often squandered, leaving the descendants of wealthy people spiritually impoverished and morally compromised.

Rabbi Daniel Lapin's delightful book, *Thou Shalt Prosper*, expands the meaning of "treasure" to include the moral and ethical training of one's children. He warns that inherited financial wealth often destroys families that lack such training.

Of course, the most important aspect of this training is the parent's behavior. What one models is more important than what one says.

Since none of us are perfect, modeling repentance must be part of how we transmit the "treasure" of moral living.

Just as families can increase their financial wealth over generations, it is also possible to increase their moral capital. My children are aware of my shortcomings. Although I wish I had lived a more upright life, they know that I deeply regret my mistakes. Hopefully, my mistakes will help them to live more fulfilling and God-centered lives than I have lived.

One of the blessings of my older life has been watching my children assume some responsibility that was once mine. Two of my sons work directly in the accounting firm that I founded. However, all of them are involved in some aspect of managing my estate and, increasingly, helping me manage my personal affairs.

When the apostle Peter was young and impetuous, the Lord Jesus told him that, although he walked where he wanted to go and did what he wished to do, days would come when that would not be the case. Peter didn't know exactly what the Lord was saying until he was much older. Indeed, the Bible says that Peter only fully learned this when he was preparing to die.

If we're fortunate enough to live a long life, we become increasingly aware of the right and wrong decisions we have made in life. We also begin to understand how our influence on our children growing up as we were going about our lives, shaped them.

In our line of work, we naturally think about our financial legacy. That requires a clear plan for transferring our physical assets into the care of others. Usually, our children and grandchildren

We are not naturally inclined to remember that our intangible resources are the ones that most impact our decendants. How many times have we witnessed the younger members of a family inherit the wealth of their parents and grandparents without the knowledge, wisdom, and integrity to manage that wealth responsibly?

Praying for our children, our spouses, and other family members is very important.

Both the Old and the New covenant begin with the family.

The Old covenant begins with Abraham, Isaac, and Jacob. The Hebrew scriptures revolve around the ways Abraham's family through the centuries got some things right and other things wrong.

The New covenant begins when God calls a woman out from her village as "blessed among women." God then assures Joseph of Mary's unique calling and invites him to join that calling. Every Christmas, we celebrate the events surrounding this young family and invite people everywhere to join that family.

In a sense, Christianity is an extension of the work of Mary, Joseph, and Jesus. The twelve disciples were the first ones to join that special family. Since then, those of us who call ourselves the followers of Christ have joined as well.

Family businesses are rather like this. They begin with long hours, over many years, in which a family invests their time and energy into providing some service or product to humanity. One often notes that the strength and weaknesses of a family business are the very strengths and weaknesses of its founding family. That's why maintaining a family's material resources is never enough to establish its legacy.

Like all children, mine have observed both the strengths and dysfunctions of their family of origin over the decades. Since we're all flawed, we don't have the option of offering our children perfection. However, I have tried to model the importance of prayer in both my home and business. Because of this, I have some reasonable assurance that my children will do better than I have in both their personal and professional lives.

Sometimes, in my prayer, I remember the apostle John saying that he had no greater joy than to know that his children walked in the truth.

That is what we mean by legacy.

PRAYER:

O Rock of Ages,

My life is but a brief flight through the world. As I prepare for the life to come, help me to live that my actions will survive me, bringing joy and comfort to the part of the world in which you have placed me.

Just as I have benefited from the gifts and examples of those who preceded me, may I do for those who come after me, and so be unashamed on that day when I join the communion of saints. Through Jesus Christ our Lord.

Amen

REFLECTION:

_____
_____
_____
_____
_____
_____
_____
_____
_____
_____
_____

Stability

30

Be still, my soul; the Lord is on thy side.
Bear patiently the cross of grief or pain.
Leave to thy God to order and provide.
In every change, He faithful will remain.
Be still, my soul—thy best, thy Heavenly Friend
Through thorny ways leads to a joyful end.

"Be Still, My Soul" by Katharina von Schlegel[1]

In the sixth century, an Italian monk named Benedict wrote a short book about serving God. One of the attributes he believed characterized those who dedicated their lives to service was stability.

He urged his readers to serve the same group of people over a long period in the same place. He didn't mean that one should never move, but simply that one should be very cautious about moving often, either geographically or between communities.

We often believe that moving allows us to start over and obtain a better life for ourselves. Sometimes, we're right about that. Moving from my home in Southern West Virginia to Tennessee was a good move, for both me and my future family.

However, doing that once or twice is one thing. Doing it often can hinder us from going deeper into our relationships with others.

As Benedict himself said, principles like stability cannot be defined in the same way for everyone. The apostle Paul moved from place to place around the Mediterranean because God directed him to do so. We could hardly accuse him of being unstable.

Alvin Toffler's book *Future Shock* was a bestseller in 1970 because he predicted that the pace of change was about to accelerate beyond our capacity to process it. Changes that once occurred over a hundred years or more would now happen in a decade. In another fifty years, he said, that same amount of change would occur in five years. In sixty years, those changes would occur yearly.

If anything, Toffler's predictions were too cautious. Nearly every part of our lives is filled with constant, unrelenting change. That means that we must remain stable amid all the adaptations we make to keep up.

Katharina von Schlegel wrote the hymn "Be Still My Soul" in 1752. Looking back, it's easy to imagine that life was much simpler and more predictable then. However, then as now, war and pestilence might come at any moment. Like us, people sometimes looked longingly at the past, believing their time was more turbulent and unpredictable than before.

The power of this hymn, based on Luke 21:19 and Psalm 131:2, rests on the line "in every change He faithful will remain." We find our stability, in other words, in God, the unmoved mover.

Quakers call this attachment of one's soul to God "peace at the center." It refers to a believer's ability to move through the storms of life to the calm at the eye of the storm. As the winds blow everything this way and that, one remains confident in the God who works everything for our good.

Psalm 131:2 (ESV) says, "I have calmed and quieted my soul, like a weaned child with its mother."

Luke 21:19 (ESV) says, "By your endurance you will gain your lives."

This hymn teaches us to speak peace into our souls by drawing on these core ideas. We remind ourselves that we are anchored in the God of eternity.

PRAYER:

Lord of all comfort,

Speak peace to my soul. Through all the vicissitudes of life, anchor my heart to the steady, unshakable Rock of Ages. Because I am so prone to shake when the world moves in ways I did not anticipate, I know I cannot remain firm without your help. Help me to hold fast to that peace at the center, that I may at last reach the safe harbor you have promised to all those who love Thee. Through Jesus Christ our Lord.

Amen

REFLECTION:

_____

_____

_____

_____

_____

_____

_____

_____

_____

A Lifelong Journey

31

"And let us not grow weary of doing good, for in due season we will reap, if we do not give up."

Galatians 6:9, ESV

The central idea of Eugene Peterson's book, *A Long Obedience in the Same Direction*[1], is that the ideas, practices, and communities to which we remain committed form us into the persons we become.

The child can imagine himself as a fireman, policeman, clergyman, or president of the country. These are all reasonable images for his future self. However, as he grows older, his choices narrow. Otherwise, none of his imagined futures will be realized.

One ultimately claims a vocation. After that, the vocation claims the person. Sometimes, that vocation claims the entire family. An accountant may be interested in English literature, physics, or oceanography.

However, these other interests must become hobbies, sidelines to the work on which we have chosen to focus most of our time. If we find we are unable to do this, we will likely make a vocational change to accommodate our true interests.

In the past, it was almost certain that a family would follow the same vocation over many generations. As a result, many family names emerged from the vocation of one's ancestors, such as Goldsmith, Cooper, Miller, Baker, Fisher, and Carpenter.

The point is that financial vocations, like all vocations, shape those who work in them. As believers, we want to actively participate in this formation of ourselves in ways that are consistent with our faith. We want to become, in other words, lifelong learners.

Most people grow weary of their chosen vocation from time to time. The movie *Mr. Holland's Opus*[2] follows the career of a musician who takes a job as a high school music teacher. He figures that he will remain at the job until he makes his great breakthrough as a composer.

As the years pass, he slowly realizes that his "great American opus" has been a fantasy. This bitter reality gives way to a revelation of what he has done in life: shaped the lives of countless young men and women.

Mr. Holland was obedient in the same direction, year after year. His opus becomes the influence for good he has radiated into the world.

We are not the ultimate judges of the positive and negative influences of our lives. The righteous Judge of All Things will render that verdict at the end of days. Our calling is merely to remain faithful day after day, year after year, allowing our choices and the challenges of life to shape us in ways that please God and bless the world.

While writing this book, my wife, Candace, gave me a prayer journal by Dr. Michelle Bengtson. It is called *Today is Going to Be a Good Day*[3]. She offers a paragraph or two to begin each day assuring the reader that whatever occurs, the Lord has promised to make "all things work together for good." (Romans 8:28)

Many writers of the past called this perspective "living in the light of eternity." As we come to the end of a day filled with challenges, it can seem that "all hell has broken loose." That is precisely when we must recapture the eternal perception and turn things over to God.

In his song "Abide with Me,"[4] hymn writer Henry Lyte, turned his own questions into a famous lyric:

> *Abide with me, fast falls the eventide*
> *The darkness deepens Lord, with me abide*
> *When other helpers fail and comforts flee*
> *Help of the helpless, oh, abide with me.*

Growing older, I often feel the approach of that evening when I will close my eyes for the last time on this earth. So, I understand why Lyte, who saw that day approaching for himself, prayed these powerful words:

> *I fear no foe, with Thee at hand to bless*
> *Ills have no weight, and tears no bitterness*
> *Where is death's sting?*
> *Where, grave, thy victory?*
> *I triumph still, if Thou abide with me.*
>
> *Hold Thou Thy cross before my closing eyes*
> *Shine through the gloom and point me to the skies*
> *Heaven's morning breaks, and earth's vain*
> *   shadows flee*
> *In life, in death, o Lord, abide with me*
> *Abide with me, abide with me.*

My prayer for you is that you will live, serve, and pray within that eternal perspective. Both good and challenging days move you toward the moment when you will account for how you have stewarded your gifts, opportunities, and the resources of others.

Rather than a sense of dread, may that awareness cultivate in you a determination to be, as much as is in your power, a righteous and just steward.

PRAYER:

Heavenly Father,

Please use both the boredom and excitement, the loneliness and the social interaction, of my vocation to shape me in ways that bless Thee and others.

Finally, in that day when you call me into eternity, may my eyes behold you clearly when I look upon your face. Through Jesus Christ our Lord.

Amen

REFLECTION:

_____

_____

_____

_____

_____

_____

_____

_____

_____

_____

_____

CPA PRAYER ALLIANCE

Our mission is to advocate and spread the message and teachings on the power of prayer and the kingdom impact it has on the lives of financial professionals, their families, their clients, and the work of their hands.

Learn more at
CPAPrayer.org

Notes

FOREWORD

1. F. Scott Fitzgerald, *The Great Gatsby* (New York: Charles Scribner's Sons, 1925), 2.

1. PRAYER

1. Heschel, Abraham Joshua. *Man's Quest for God: Studies in Prayer and Symbolism.* New York: Scribner, 1954.
2. Cowper, William. *God Moves in a Mysterious Way.* 1774.
3. Askins, George. *Brethren, We Have Met to Worship.* 1819.

2. PRACTICE

1. *Just a Closer Walk with Thee.* Traditional gospel hymn, 19th century.

11. PLANNING

1. *I Know Who Holds Tomorrow* (CMG Song #80028), written by Ira F. Stanphill, Copyright © 1950, New Spring Publishing Inc. (ASCAP) (administered at CapitolCMG-Publishing.com). All rights reserved. Used by permission.

12. JOY

1. *The Journals of Father Alexander Schmemann* (St. Vladimir's Press), p. 129.

18. TRUST

1. Louisa M. R. Stead, "'Tis So Sweet to Trust in Jesus," 1882. Public Domain.

23. FORGIVENESS

1. *"Wilt Thou Forgive?"* by **John Donne** (1572–1631) is in the **public domain worldwide**. It may be freely copied, modified, and distributed without restriction.

24. TIMING

1. Bounds, E. M., Andrew Murray, and John Wesley. *Prayer Is the Answer: Classic Writings on Prayer.* 2018.

27. FORMATION

1. *"Sweet Hour of Prayer"*
   Lyrics by William W. Walford, c. 1845
   Music by William B. Bradbury, 1861
   This hymn is in the **public domain** worldwide. Originally published before **1929**, and with its authors deceased for over **70 years**, it is no longer under copyright protection. It may be freely used, reproduced, and distributed without restriction.

30. STABILITY

1. Katharina von Schlegel, *Be Still, My Soul*, 1752, trans. Jane Laurie Borthwick, 1855, set to *Finlandia* by Jean Sibelius, 1899–1900.
   Public Domain Notice:
   This hymn is in the **public domain worldwide**. It may be freely used, reproduced, and distributed without restriction.

31. A LIFELONG JOURNEY

1. Peterson, Eugene H. *A Long Obedience in the Same Direction: Discipleship in an Instant Society.* Downers Grove, IL: InterVarsity Press, 2000.
2. Pellington, Stephen, dir. *Mr. Holland's Opus.* Burbank, CA: Walt Disney Pictures, 1995.
3. Bengtson, Michelle. *Today Is Going to Be a Good Day: 90 Promises from God to Start Your Day Off Right.* Grand Rapids, MI: Revell, 2022.
4. Lyte, Henry Francis. *Abide with Me.* 1847. Music by William H. Monk, 1861.

NOTES

Note: Hymns in the public domain do not require formal citation but should include attribution.